Biological Foundations of Behaviour

D0145697

Open Guides to Psychology

Series Editor: Judith Greene, Professor of Psychology at the Open University

Titles in the series

Learning to Use Statistical Tests in Psychology
Judith Greene and Manuela D'Oliveira

Basic Cognitive Processes
Judith Greene and Carolyn Hicks

Memory: A Cognitive Approach
Gillian Cohen, Michael W. Eysenck and Martin E. Le Voi

Language Understanding: A Cognitive Approach
Judith Green

Problem Solving: A Cognitive Approach
Hank Kahney

Perception and Representation: A Cognitive Approach
Ilona Roth and John Frisby

Designing and Reporting Experiments
Peter Harris

Biological Foundations of Behaviour
Frederick Toates

Titles in preparation

Basic Social Psychology
Dorothy Miell

Biological Foundations of Behaviour

Frederick Toates

Open University Press
Milton Keynes · Philadelphia

Open University Press
Open University Education Enterprises Limited
12 Cofferidge Close
Stony Stratford
Milton Keynes MK11 1BY, England

and
242 Cherry Street,
Philadelphia, PA 19106. USA

First Published 1986

British Library Cataloguing in Publication Data

Toates, Frederick
  Biological foundations of behaviour.
  (Open guides to psychology)
  1. Psychology, Physiological
  I. Title   II. Series
  152   QP360

  ISBN 0-335-15333-X

Library of Congress Cataloging in Publication Data

Main entry under title
Toates, F. M. (Frederick M.)
  Biological Foundations of Behaviour.
  (Open guides to psychology)
  Bibliography: p.
  Includes index.
  1. Neuropsychology. I. Title. II. Series: Open
guides to psychology series.
  DNLM: 1. Behaviour—physiology. 2. Nervous system—physiology.
  3. Psychophysiology.
  WL 103 T627B
  QP360.T63 1986 152 86-5158
  ISBN 0-335-15333-X (pbk.)

Typeset by Mathematical Composition Setters, Salisbury, UK
Printed in Great Britian by Biddles Ltd, Guildford.

Contents

Contents

Preface

The aim of this Open Guide to Psychology is to provide revision material for courses in the area of biology, brain and behaviour. The revision materials cover the areas of the nerve cell, neuronal systems, learning and memory, motivation and theoretical issues in brain and behaviour. This is core material of the area, though it is not claimed to be an exhaustive coverage. The reader should, however, be able to gain here sufficient impression of the relationships between biology, brain and behaviour such as to enable other topics in this area to be better approached. This book contains the essential facts in summary form and provides a framework around which to organize revision, using the teaching techniques that have proved successful with Open University students, including Diagnostic Questions, Key Notes and Methodology Notes.

For Whom Is the Book Intended?

Perhaps it is important to stress that the Open Guides to Psychology are not designed to give training in the techniques needed to practise in, say, clinical psychology. What they do offer are specially designed revision programmes to ensure successful performance in the courses which are necessary prerequisites for further specialized training.

The series of revision guides are intended to cover the main areas of psychology. The present guide enjoys perhaps a unique position in the series, as follows. The area of biology, brain and behaviour described here forms an essential part of many psychology courses. However, the material is equally applicable to other areas, such as medicine, nursing, biology and ethology. It is hoped that students within contexts other than psychology might equally find the material useful.

We hope, too, that teachers of courses in psychology and other areas might find this Open Guide useful for structuring the topic and providing many worked-through examples.

Students taking the Open University course SD286, Biology, Brain and Behaviour, would be expected to find the book useful. However, it must be emphasized that it is not a substitute for the material contained within the course, nor is it a set book. Rather, it is an optional *addition* to this course.

Acknowledgements

The original inspiration for this guide was, in large part, the Open University course Biology, Brain and Behaviour (SD286), written by a course team from the Science and Social Science faculties. What follows is my own interpretation of how to revise material such as that comprising this course. I am grateful to the course team for their help to me in producing a personal interpretation of this area, and for permission to use many of the original figures from the course. Naturally, my own particular way of viewing the material differs to some extent from that of other members of the course team. For example, the present writer is more sympathetic to Skinnerian behaviourism and other unpopular causes than are some of his associates. What I have attempted to do is to give a fair and balanced account of the available evidence. I should like to record my thanks to those people who read the first draft of the book and provided masses of invaluable assistance: Michel Cabanac of the Université Claude Bernard, Lyon; Helen Boyce and Judith Greene of the Open University; John Skelton of Open University Press; and Robin Orchardson of the University of Glasgow. I am also most grateful to Dr Patrick Murphy of the West Midlands Regional Office of the Open University for his generous assistance in teaching me how to use a word-processor, the benefit of which I hope is reflected in the pages that follow. Finally, I would like to thank Mr. Derek Parker for his fine attention to detail in going through the finished product.

How to Use this Guide

The aim of this book is to provide you with a guide to the essential information you will need in order to take an examination on the general topic of Biology, Brain and Behaviour. Examination papers in this area go under a variety of different names, such as that just given as well as Biological Foundations of Behaviour, and Biological Bases of Behaviour.

The book attempts to summarize the essence of the relationships between biology, brain and behaviour. In so doing, it emphasizes caution. It is all too easy to rush in with biological explanations of any interesting social phenomenon. The philosophy of the book is that biology is indispensable in understanding behaviour, but that we must avoid naive uses of biology.

The Six Modules

The book is organized into six modules to cover the following: (1) introduction and discussion of types of explanation in biology, brain and behaviour; (2) the neuron; (3) neuronal systems; (4) learning and memory; (5) motivation; and (6) theoretical issues in brain and behaviour. This division is to some extent arbitrary: learning and memory involve neuronal systems, and learning plays a crucial role in motivation. However, one must simplify and classify phenomena in order to describe and explain them. The divisions made here are ones that are commonly encountered in the literature. Cross-referencing between modules should help to get a more integrated view of the subject. However, we should not try to disguise the fact that real differences of opinion and research philosophy do sometimes appear. For example, B.F. Skinner (described in Module 6) would regard attempts to explain behaviour by appealing to cognitive or neural mechanisms as being essentially a waste of time. Conversely, ethologists might regard Skinner's techniques for analysing behaviour as being hopelessly restrictive.

Techniques Boxes and Methodology Notes

A source of some confusion to students is the multiplicity of techniques and experimental designs used in the brain and behavioural sciences. To help you here we have included a few Techniques Boxes that briefly describe the experimental technique employed. The Methodology Notes explain general principles of how to go about designing good experiments, and relate back to issues arising in the earlier sections of the book.

Index of Concepts and References

In order to help you find your way around the book, there is an Index of Concepts which lists all of the concepts described in the text. The page numbers refer you back to where each concept was defined (shown in italics in the text).

There is also a References Section, which gives the authors of books and articles.

Diagnostic Questions

Since the book is an 'Open Guide', it is essential that you should take an active part in assimilating the text rather than being a passive receiver of information. After all, you are perhaps the best person to diagnose what you already know and what you need to learn.

Each module starts with General Diagnostic Questions. In each case, there is an indication of which section of the text is particularly helpful for answering each question, although, of course, you should attempt to see the relevance of other sections of the Guide. At the end of each module, you will benefit from going back to the general diagnostic questions to see whether you now feel competent to tackle them.

The Key Notes at the end of each section summarize the essential points made in that section. You should make sure that you understand these summaries and the evidence on which they are based. Finally, go back to the beginning of the section and look at the Diagnostic Questions.

Self-Assessment Questions (SAQs)

It is essential that you attempt to answer each of the Self-Assessment Questions (SAQs) before you look up the answers at the back of the book. These SAQs are designed to test your understanding of theories and methodologies described in the text. It is strongly advised that you do not jump over the SAQs.

Suggestions for Reading

Each module has a Reading Guide that suggests some general reading. References are made to Open University texts that contain further information about the various topics, and other books that you should find helpful are listed. Recommended books include some modules of the Open University course *SD286 Biology, Brain and Behaviour* (these are obtainable from Open University Educational Enterprises, Milton Keynes).

1 Introduction Module

General Diagnostic Questions for the Introduction

1. Briefly state why, and how, we might approach the explanation of a given phenomenon by investigations at more than one level. (Sect. 1.1.)
2. Is it possible to believe in both reductionism and holism? (Sect. 1.2.)
3. In what way can a causal explanation be used to account for the behaviour of an individual animal? (Sect. 1.3.)
4. What role do action potentials play in the life of an animal? (Sect. 1.4.)
5. Very briefly describe some of the events that occur in the execution of a simple reflex. (Sect. 1.5.)
6. Give two examples of why caution is needed in the interpretation of evidence on brain anatomy and function. (Sect. 1.6.)

1.1 Levels of Explanation

Diagnostic Questions for Section 1.1

1. Describe the range of disciplines concerned with the study of brain and behaviour.
2. Is it possible for a discipline to study a phenomenon at just one level, or does it need to look to a lower-level discipline for explanations?
3. Can there be more than one way of explaining a given phenomenon?

A subject that will occupy us throughout this book is the possible relationships between biology and behaviour. Both animals and humans will be discussed, and we shall look at several different types of explanatory principle. Our main focus for explanations will be the *nervous system* and its role in the organization of behaviour.

In one way or another, a very wide range of disciplines is concerned with brain and behaviour. Figure 1.1 illustrates this range, indicating the appropriate domains for each discipline. Somewhere in the mid-range of the scale we have the nervous system. The nervous system is made up of millions of nerve cells, termed *neurons*. The study of such cells and their mode of interconnection falls

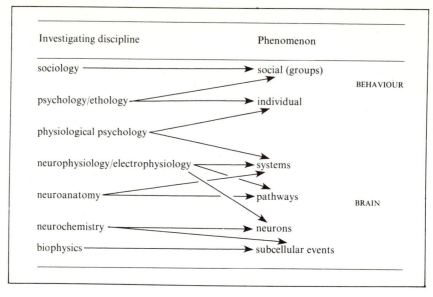

Figure 1.1 Table illustrating the phenomena and disciplines of the brain and behavioural sciences.
(Source: SD286, Module A.)

mainly within the domains of neurophysiology and neuroanatomy. However, some researchers represented in Figure 1.1 study events at an even 'finer grain', looking at the components and make-up of individual cells. This is within the domain of biophysics and biochemistry (more specifically, *neurochemistry* in the present context). Moving above neurophysiology we find psychology and ethology, the latter being concerned with the behaviour of animals in their natural environment. At the top of the scale there are social psychology and sociology, concerned with the behaviour of humans in groups.

The discipline scale does not represent relative academic worth nor scientific respectability. More than anything else, the relative locations depend upon the *size* of the system under study. A system can be defined as a collection of parts organized by some identifiable principle, and thereby forming an object of study (Hardy and Stolwijk, 1968; Cabanac and Russek, 1982). For example, we have the solar system, consisting of the planets, or the circulatory system, made up of the heart, blood and blood vessels, and so on. To view social psychology in such terms, the parts of the system would be individual humans and the system would consist of these individuals and their social interactions. For the neurochemist, sometimes the parts might well be as small as molecules forming part of the 'system' of a nerve cell.

SAQ 1
Justify the ordering of disciplines and phenomena in the table of Figure 1.1. (For answers to SAQs, see p. 117).

How do the various disciplines share responsibility, and what is the relationship between them? To answer this we can either start with a given *phenomenon* (e.g. a particular instance of behaviour) or the investigating discipline. By either route we will usually arrive at the conclusion that there can be more than one plausible way of explaining a given situation. The nature of how we construct our explanation depends upon our *purpose* in making it; that is, what we are trying to achieve at the end of the explanation.

To understand the issue of types of explanation, let us take psychology as an example. Generally speaking, psychology is concerned with understanding whole living *organisms*, whether these are humans, rats or sea slugs. Sometimes it is claimed that psychologists see their favourite subjects, rats, as simplified and manageable versions of humans. Whether using rats or humans, the test environment is usually made simple, so that the behavioural possibilities are severely limited. Nonetheless, the object of the exercise is to explain the behaviour of a *whole* organism; for example, we might ask: why is the rat eating and not drinking?

For the moment, we shall consider just two kinds of explanation, though others will be discussed later. These are (1) explanations at the psychological level (i.e. keeping within just one level in the table) and (2) explanations that make use of information at a lower level, in this case neurophysiology. As an example of where explanations keeping within the psychological domain can be offered, consider the position adopted by the American behaviourist B. F. Skinner. Skinner has been very successful in demonstrating how the behaviour of rats and pigeons can be brought under the control of their environment. In order to change behaviour, Skinnerians apply reinforcement (e.g. pellets of food) for behaviours that approximate to the behaviour desired by the experimenter. In such an experiment, the animal would typically have been food-deprived, so that food constitutes a reinforcer. Skinner claims to have demonstrated a ubiquitous property of living systems, such that principles of reinforcement can be employed even to cure the ills of human society (see Sect. 6.3). For example, if a child is repeatedly disruptive in class, despite being sent out of class, a Skinnerian might explain this in terms of the positive reinforcement derived from meeting friends in the corridor.

As a psychologist Skinner expresses no interest in probing beneath the skin. Rather, he believes that psychology must remain a science in its own right, not appealing to lower-level events. For example, Skinner is not concerned with explaining *why* water is a reinforcer to a thirsty rat, or *why* the child finds friends in the corridor attractive: it is sufficient to know that both constitute reinforcers that enable behaviour to be shaped (i.e. modified by its consequences).

Now let us contrast Skinner's position with that of physiological psychology, a so-called *bridge-discipline*. With an eye to explaining behaviour, the physiological psychologist will examine how particular collections of neurons work, or how a certain hormone affects the nervous system. The assumption is that internal events, on the one level, play a role in generating (at a higher level) behaviour.

What considerations determine our research methods? When might one employ the techniques of physiological psychology as opposed to those of a behavioural psychologist like Skinner? The question is best answered by specific examples. Suppose a psychologist were called in by a school to suggest how classroom disruption can be minimized. The psychologist might start by observing behaviours and their consequences in order to see whether there are any obvious environmental manipulations that could be recommended. It is difficult to see that anything useful would be derived from looking at the brains of the pupils.

Suppose, though, that a psychologist has been asked to give advice on a safe and cheap substitute for heroin, so as to enable addicts to break their habit. Such factors as how rapidly the drug is taken up by the brain and how rapidly it is broken down might need investigation. Correlations between brain levels of the drug and subjective reports of euphoria might be useful. A knowledge of the effect of the drug on the nervous system could yield vital predictions on the likely duration of any euphoria, and whether aversive withdrawal effects might follow. Such an analysis demands expertise from more than one discipline and consideration of how events in the nervous system relate to subjective states.

Note that within-discipline and between-discipline approaches are not mutually exclusive. At least in principle, a given phenomenon might be explicable by either method. Take, for example, a rat that has been trained to press a bar for food. Then the food is omitted, and after a while the rat stops pressing the lever. Why? One might refer to a very general property of behavioural control by positive reinforcement, which is that when such reinforcement is omitted, the behaviour it was previously supporting gradually weakens. Such an explanation would be useful in that it would enable one to reject other possible explanations of why the rat is not bar-pressing, for example, it might have gorged itself on cakes just before the experiment. However, if we wanted to probe the nervous system, it is possible that we could identify a change in activity of certain neurons previously playing a vital role in the generation of bar-pressing.

SAQ 2
Are levels of explanation in terms of events at a lower level more useful than within-level explanations?

Key Notes 1.1

1. We can explain phenomena either by keeping within one level of investigation or by looking at events at a different (often lower) level.
2. The choice of which explanatory approach to adopt is heavily dependent upon one's purpose in making the explanation.

1.2   Reductionism and Holism

Diagnostic Questions for Section 1.2

1. What is meant by the terms 'reductionism' and 'holism'?
2. Is reductionism inherently a naive way of trying to understand the behaviour of a complex system?
3. What is an 'emergent property'?

We noted in the previous section that we can often gain useful insight by looking at events occurring at a level below that at which the phenomenon of interest occurs (see Fig. 1.1). This approach is known as *reductionism*. The success associated with such lower-level investigation might suggest that we should attempt to explain *all* of what occurs at one level in terms of events at a lower level. For example, in order to explain psychological phenomena, we might focus exclusively upon the various parts of the nervous system. Having an understanding of the neural components, we would have solved the issues of psychology. Psychologists should simply hand over their research programmes to their associates in neurophysiology.

I have deliberately played devil's advocate by advancing the most extreme form of reductionism. Few would subscribe to such a radical programme of reductionism. There are a number of reasons why this is so. In psychology, much as we might successfully exploit a knowledge of neurophysiology, we still need to consider how such mechanisms act in the context of the whole organism interacting with its larger environment. No matter how well we understand the bits, at a higher level there will be a need for a body of theory dealing with how the *whole* system functions. There is absolutely no reason to believe that neurophysiologists would be better than psychologists as the custodians of this body of theory. Neither have we reason to believe that they have enough time to take on the task, so psychologists are likely to retain their place in the sun. In fact, there is little point in saying any more about the kind of naive reductionism that believes each discipline should swallow up that immediately above it in the table, until presumably we all become nuclear physicists. The approach to explanation that is opposite to naive reductionism, and makes the central assumption that each level has properties peculiar to itself, is known as *holism*. It is sometimes said that properties *emerge* at each level, and such emergence is encompassed by the notion of holism. What is meant by the term *emergent property* can be rather well illustrated by a very simple, but vivid, example provided by engineering science.

Consider the shape of the reaction shown by the capacitor in Figure 1.2a when an electrical voltage is applied to it. Now compare this with the reaction that an inductor shows to the same stimulus (Fig. 1.2b). Having established the response characteristics of two components, it is revealing to see what happens when we put them together to form a system. Figure 1.2c shows the response of such a system to the same stimulus as applied to the individual components. An oscillation *emerges* as the response of the system. Note that the oscillation is in no way evident in the response of either component on its own.

It is not partly present in the response of one component and partly evident also in the response of the other. It is a property of their mode of interconnection. It is true that an engineer, having a knowledge of the characteristics of each component and also an understanding of circuits, could predict the oscillation. However, the example makes very clear the pitfalls of naively looking at the response of the components on their own as the source of all understanding. If you can show emergent properties with a couple of electrical components, consider how rich are the possibilities for such emergence from the human nervous system in interaction with its environment.

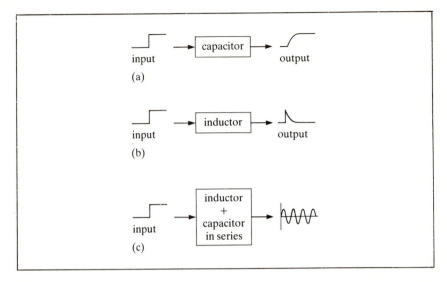

Figure 1.2   Electrical system. (a) Reaction of a capacitor to a step change in the electrical voltage applied across it. (b) Reaction of an inductor to the same input. (c) Reaction of a circuit consisting of the two components, capacitor and inductor, to the step change in input.

SAQ 3
How might the notion of emergent properties be related to the relationship between the psychology of individuals and social psychology?

Despite our rejection of naive reductionism, we cannot make the general assumption that reductionism is inherently bad. Carefully qualified reductionism, searching for the role of lower-level events, in the context of a higher-level understanding, is to be encouraged. For example, at the level of biochemistry and the nerve cell, we have a rather good understanding of the role of the substance lignocaine (a local anaesthetic) in alleviating the pain evoked by, say, a dentist's drill. However, we can only fully appreciate the pain and its alleviation in the context of the whole pain system.

SAQ 4
Suppose there exists a statue that all admire for its beauty. Then, one day, vandals knock off its nose. People then say that the statue is no longer beautiful. From this, might we conclude that beauty resides in the nose?

7

The explanation of a phenomenon at one level in terms of the characteristics of components at a lower level is sometimes known as a *bottom-up* approach. It reflects the traditional reductionist mode of explanation. However, for other explanatory purposes we are equally entitled to use the opposite direction of explanation: *top-down*. This is an holistic approach, which enables the activity of a component to be understood in terms of the larger system of which it forms a part. Suppose we ask: why are the muscles in the leg of a person particularly active at a certain point in time? A logical explanation that could prove useful is that the person is fleeing from a charging bull. Such fleeing and the associated muscular activity depend logically upon the whole man, bull and environment interaction. The answer in terms of the bull is viable for certain explanatory purposes. For other purposes we would need to explain fleeing in terms of the activity of the leg muscles. No one approach has a monopoly of the truth; several different explanations can co-exist, a message that forms the essence of the approach adopted here.

Key Notes 1.2

1. Naive reductionism is to be avoided.
2. Explaining phenomena in terms of events at a lower level can often prove very useful, though any such explanation should take into account properties of the whole system of which the lower-level event forms a part.
3. Holism is an approach that emphasizes that properties emerge at each level, peculiar to that level. For some purposes one can usefully employ whole-system properties to explain the behaviour of the components of a system.

1.3 Functional and Causal Explanations

Diagnostic Questions for Section 1.3

1. How can a given phenomenon be explained in two very different .ways, depending upon whether a causal or functional explanation is required?
2. Does a functional explanation imply that the animal can consciously perceive a goal?

In a somewhat different context, we shall now return to the theme that there can be more than one equally good explanation for a given phenomenon. Earlier, whether or not we atempted reduction to a lower level, we were concerned only with what are traditionally known as *causal* explanations. For example, owing to its action on the nervous system, aspirin might be said to *cause* a lowering of pain. First, there is the action of aspirin and, as a consequence, the diminution of pain. Similarly, in the case of the Skinner-box, one might say that the omission of food *causes* the animal to terminate bar-pressing activity. This section compares the causal level of explanation with what is known as the *functional* level. The distinction can perhaps be best illustrated by taking a specific example from the experimental literature.

Suppose a male rat is first food-deprived and then placed in the presence of both food and a sexually receptive female rat. Brown and McFarland (1979) found that, confronted with such a choice, even a severely food-deprived rat would normally mate first and eat later. In order to explain this at a causal level, we would probably start by postulating two motivational states arising in the nervous system. One would be influenced by sex hormones and would play a role in the instigation of sexual behaviour. The other would be a feeding motivational state and would be influenced by such things as the animal's current state of energy balance and the quality of available food (see Module 5 for details). We would need to propose that these two motivational tendencies are in some way compared in the nervous system and, sexual motivation, being the stronger, dominates. Such is the causal approach to explanation.

In order to pose a functional question, we would ask what factors in the animal's evolutionary history might have played a role in determining this tendency. It would make little sense when viewed in terms of *individual* survival to mate first and eat later. However, contemporary ethology now emphasizes that characteristics are selected through evolution not because of their value for individual survival *per se* but for their value in *gene perpetuation*. We might argue that, in the past, those male rats that behaved in the way just described have left a greater number of offspring, who also behaved in this way. Hence, such rats are with us today. Those adopting other strategies—for example, looking after the stomach first—have 'missed out'. This would constitute a *functional* explanation. Thus we can use both causal and functional explanations for the same behavioural phenomenon. They refer to different aspects of the same situation.

Some people like to regard the causal explanation as being a response to the question of *how* things happen as they do, whereas the functional explanation answers *why*. For some purposes such a distinction might be illuminating, but it should be used only with caution. It is possible to fall into some awful traps. Starting one's question with 'why' can lead the unwary to suppose that rats of high libido have the conscious intention of leaving their mark on posterity. Of course, such an assumption is not involved in making functional explanations. Over generations, evolutionary processes have simply favoured animals adopting certain strategies and penalized others. In other words, gene perpetuation does not *cause* an animal to mate in the sense that a loud noise causes it to flee. Loosely worded accounts of cause and effect, involving such apparently innocuous words as 'because' can lead the unwary into some pitfalls.

SAQ 5
Are functional and causal explanations competing views of what is true?

A very important assumption in ethology is that to understand fully a behaviour in a particular species we need to consider it from both functional and causal points of view. Having found a possible functional explanation for something, this can sometimes help the search for causal mechanism. However, we must take great care not to muddle bits of causal and functional levels in the same explanation. For example, in explaining why a given rat opts to copulate rather than feed, it would be misleading to say that it does so in order to gain an advantage in terms of genetic perpetuation. Unfortunately, this kind of statement is all too common.

In later sections we shall briefly return to the theme of levels and types of different explanation. For the moment the discussion returns to the nervous system, the source of so much of our evidence concerning behaviour. We shall describe the fundamental components of the nervous system and how a knowledge of such components can be exploited.

Key Notes 1.3

1. Functional and causal explanations are responses to questions concerning different aspects of a given behavioural situation.
2. Functional explanations refer to evolutionary processes, not conscious wishes.

1.4   The Nerve Cell

Diagnostic Questions for Section 1.4

1. What is a cell?
2. For what specific function is the nerve cell specialized?
3. What is the 'language' commonly employed by nerve cells to convey information?

This section looks at how we go about investigating the individual nerve cell, and what kind of information has been gained. Such knowledge is vital in understanding how collections of nerve cells form systems.

The body is made up of millions of cells of various kinds; for example, skin, blood and nerve cells. Such cells are specialized to serve particular functions (e.g. a red blood cell transports oxygen). Despite the differences between cells, reflecting their different functions, they have certain properties in common. Thus they are all surrounded by a membrane that forms a barrier of sorts between the environments internal and external to the cell.

SAQ 6
Can you see any features in common between the cells as part of a living system and people making up a complex social organization?

The type of cell that concerns us here is the nerve cell, or as it is more usually called, the *neuron*. Neurons come in various shapes and sizes. Normally a neuron has an identifiable *cell body* and one or more *processes* extending out from this body. The expression 'nerve' usually refers to a collection of individual neurons formed into a bundle. The *nervous system* is made up of millions of neurons. Those located in the *brain* and *spinal cord* together constitute a special division of the nervous system, termed the *central nervous system* (CNS) (Fig. 1.3). The purpose of each neuron is to carry a signal. The distance over which information is carried can vary from a fraction of a millimetre to several metres.

Events in the external environment impinge upon the organism in various ways; for example, light falls on the eye or a sharp object damages the foot. No matter what their physical form, to be detectable such events need to influence the nervous system. In some cases, *sensory organs*, such as the eye and nose, are specialized to perform such an operation.

As an initial stage of detection, sensory information will need to *activate* a nerve cell somewhere; for example, when the hand touches

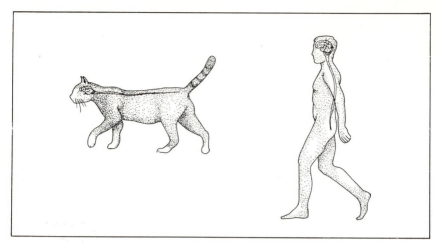

Figure 1.3 The brain and spinal cord shown in relation to the rest of the body.
(Source: SD286, Module A.)

a hot object, a specialized neuron will detect any tissue damage. Such neurons run betwen the skin and spinal cord. Detection of tissue damage at the tip of the specialized neuron is the first stage in the process leading to removal of the hand from the offending object and the conscious sensation of pain. Light hitting the retina of the eye will influence cells specialized to absorb light. This is the first stage in a process leading to perception of form.

Neurons sensitive to tissue damage are members of a class of cell that is concerned with conveying information *to* the central nervous system. This information concerns environmental events impinging upon the organism, and neurons conveying such information are known as *sensory neurons* or *afferent neurons*. Another population of neurons carries information from the central nervous system outwards to the periphery. Such neurons are termed *efferent neurons*. For example, if the brain issues the command 'move a foot', something must carry the message to the muscles controlling the foot. Neurons that deliver the commands to muscles are termed *motor neurons*.

Within the brain and spinal cord there exists a vast population of neurons that neither carry information inwards from the periphery nor convey it outwards. This is the population that we associate with, amongst other things, processing of incoming information and the determination of behavioural commands. Such neurons are known as *interneurons*.

How do neurons 'convey information'? There is more than one means, but for the moment we shall be concerned with a particular type of neuron which transmits information in the form of *action potentials*. This is the means that is invariably used when information is transmitted by a neuron over large distances (e.g. from skin to spinal cord). An action potential is an impulse of electrical activity in a neuron (see Techniques Box A). The action potential normally travels along a neuron in one direction. Information is carried along the neuron in the form of how *frequently* it transmits action potentials. For example, in a sensory neuron, a firing rate of 10 action potentials per second might correspond to a weak pressure at the skin, whereas a rate of 30 per second might be caused by a stronger pressure.

Techniques Box A

Recording the activity of a neuron

In some cases, it is possible to isolate single nerve cells and to observe their electrical activity. In Figure 1.4 the *axon*, a part of a nerve cell (described in Module 2) has been isolated. The neuron is artificially electrically stimulated by a voltage source, acting upon an electrode, whose tip is implanted in the neuron. At some distance from the stimulating electrode, the tip of a recording electrode is similarly placed within the nerve cell. This recording electrode enables any change in the electrical state of the nerve cell ('membrane potential') to be observed on a scale. If the stimulation is sufficiently strong, an action potential can be generated at the site of the electrode tip. This will then travel along the axon and will be detected by the recording apparatus. Continued stimulation will generate further action potentials, each one almost identical.

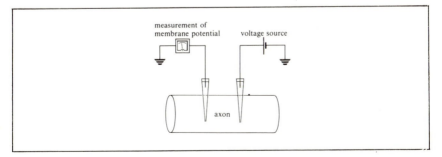

Figure 1.4   Stimulation and recording apparatus.
(Source: SD286, Module B1.)

The transmission of an action potential along a neuron is something like igniting a fuse and watching the flame run along until the explosive is ignited. Having instigated the signal, in both cases it is carried by its own momentum. Transmission of information by action potentials also has features in common with the series of dots and dashes that carry signals in Morse code.

SAQ 7
Transmission by action potentials in a neuron is, in some respects, analogous to how Morse code is transmitted along a wire. However, where does such an analogy break down?

So, to take an example, when a sharp object damages the skin, action potentials are set up at the peripheral end of a neuron specialized to detect tissue damage. A series of such action potentials is transmitted from periphery towards the spinal cord. At the spinal cord the specialized cells relay the information on tissue damage to other cells that form part of the system that might ultimately lead to the conscious perception of pain (described in Sect. 3.3).

Let us return to the subject of the variety of events in the external environment that impinge upon the organism's sense organs.

SAQ 8
Name some of the sense organs and the physical stimuli to which they respond.

Despite the rich variety of such sensory information, it is all carried along neurons to the CNS in the form of action potentials. Consider vision. The optic nerve is a bundle made up of millions of individual neurons carrying information from the eye. Signals in the optic nerve carrying information on the visual world look much the same as those in the auditory nerve responding to sounds. The difference in the sensation that you experience is not primarily because the information is coded any differently at the input side. It is *which* nerve cells fire and what parts of the brain are thereby influenced that determines which sensation is perceived.

Key Notes 1.4

1. Neurons are cells specialized to convey information
2. Afferent neurons carry information to the CNS, and efferent neurons carry it from the CNS.

3. Information is carried in the form of impulses of electrical activity, known as action potentials.
4. The frequency with which a neuron transmits action potentials is a means of conveying information, since one action potential looks much like any other.
5. The various types of sensory neurons and motor neurons all transmit very similar-looking nerve impulses.

1.5   Brain and Spinal Cord

Diagnostic Questions for Section 1.5

1. Describe briefly what sort of information enters the brain and spinal cord, and what sort leaves.
2. Outline very briefly some of the basic anatomy involved in the transfer of information described in your answer to 1. above.
3. What advantage could be served by information on tissue damage activating motor neurons at the spinal level?

Afferent nerves, having been stimulated by the presence of events in the external environment, transmit this information to the CNS. In certain pathways, information enters the brain without first entering the spinal cord (e.g. visual information; see Module 3). In other pathways, sensory information first enters the spinal cord, and then passes up to the brain. Other information passes from the brain, down the spinal cord and then out, towards the periphery. An example of the latter is motor information, running from brain to muscle.

Figure 1.5 shows a section of spinal cord. A given spinal nerve (SN) is associated with a discrete chunk (segment) of spinal cord. This spinal nerve is made up of afferent and efferent components. A 'bundle' of many individual afferent nerve fibres enters the cord as the *dorsal root nerve* (DRN). They pass into the *grey matter* of the cord (GM). Each such fibre forms part of an individual neuron. These neurons have their cell bodies located in the *dorsal root ganglion*, and an extension or 'process' (often termed the 'nerve fibre') runs from the periphery to the spinal cord. Other nerves, motor nerves, leave the cord, in a 'bundle' termed the *ventral root nerve*. The dorsal root nerve and the ventral root nerve merge to form the spinal nerve, which contains both afferent fibres (from sensory organs) and efferent fibres (supplying muscles). Nearer the periphery, the spinal nerve again divides into its afferent and efferent components.

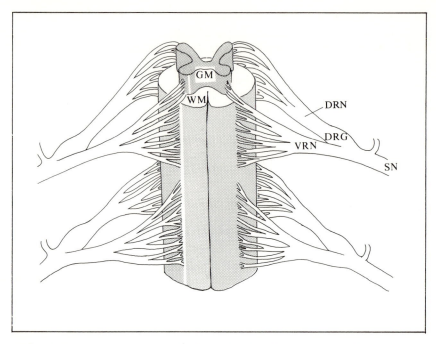

Figure 1.5 A section of spinal cord, showing the associated nerves. GM = grey matter of the spinal cord; WM = white matter of the cord; SN = a spinal nerve; VRN = ventral root nerve, DRG = dorsal root ganglion. The dorsal root ganglion is a swelling that contains the cell bodies of afferent neurons. Note that, on approaching the spinal cord, the spinal nerve diverges into two components, the VRN and DRN. Four such spinal nerves are shown here.

(Source: SD286, Module A.)

SAQ 9
Two patients are examined in a hospital. Patient A has suffered an injury which severed dorsal root nerves, whereas patient B's injury involved severing ventral root nerves. What symptoms would A and B experience?

Suppose the foot touches a sharp object. Action potentials will be set up in particular afferent neurons, and information on tissue damage will be conveyed to the spinal cord. Here, two things happen. The afferent signal will activate particular motor neurons, usually acting via a connecting interneuron (Fig. 1.6). These motor neurons activate a muscle, causing the foot to be removed from the sharp object. Also, the afferent neuron will make contact with a

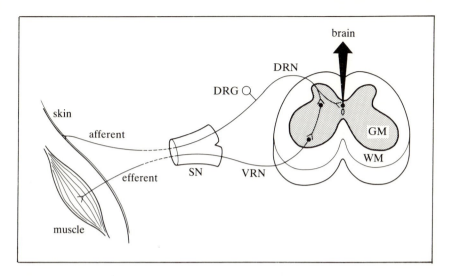

Figure 1.6   Reflex arc. An afferent neuron is shown with its tip at the skin. Action potentials arising at the tip travel inwards towards the spinal cord. A bundle of many such afferent fibres enter the cord as the dorsal root nerve (DRN). Note also the efferent neuron, leaving the spinal cord as part of the ventral root nerve (VRN) and supplying a muscle. It can be seen that between the afferent and efferent neurons an interneuron is located. Activity in the afferent neuron activates the efferent neuron via this interneuron. Note the spinal level of organization of this reflex, not involving the brain. However, a message is also sent up to the brain. Observe the location of white matter (WM) and grey matter (GM) in the spinal cord. The dorsal root ganglion (DRG) contains the cell bodies (described in Module 2) of the afferent neurons. ─<●─point of contact between two neurons.

neuron that carries the information up to the brain. The nerve fibres projecting from the spinal cord to the brain are located in the white matter (WM) of the spinal cord. The localized organization of action involving just an afferent neuron, interneuron, efferent (motor) neuron and muscle constitutes what we call a *reflex arc*. In this case, the motor response, known as a *reflex*, is a fast-acting defence mechanism to protect the body against tissue damage.

Key Notes 1.5

1. Information can enter the spinal cord, and then pass up to the brain.

2. In some cases, sensory nerves go directly to parts of the brain.
3. Some reflexes are organized at the spinal level.

1.6 Brain Anatomy and Function

Diagnostic Questions for Section 1.6

1. Describe some of the techniques that can be used to study the functions of the brain and the kind of information that their use might reveal.
2. What is meant by the expression 'pleasure centre'?
3. Why might our definition of what constitutes the association cortex be described as a negative one?

This section presents a brief account of some of the methods by which we can attempt to gain an understanding of the relationships between brain structure and function. It will illustrate some of the pitfalls to be avoided in making such explanations.

The brain receives information concerning the external environment via sensory nerves. The internal chemical environment of the body also influences brain function. Behaviour is executed via commands generated in the brain and transmitted via motor neurons to the muscles. The brain sciences occupy themselves with the question: how does the brain process information? Also: what is the function of the different brain regions in the processing of information? We need to ask to what extent we can allocate responsibility for a particular behavioural feature to particular brain regions. As will become apparent later, we need to be very cautious in any such allocations of responsibility, recognizing that simple one-to-one mapping will almost certainly be proven wrong. What we can do is, whilst acknowledging the complexity of brain activity involved in any behaviour, attempt to find regions of particular importance for a given behaviour. We can ask what the role of a particular region appears to be, even though we know that it cannot act in isolation (remember the discussion of emergent properties in Sect. 1.2).

Our understanding of brain anatomy and function has been gained in various ways. One kind of evidence is provided by brain damage through accidents, such as those received in war. One can examine the extent of the damage, or *lesion*, and attempt to compare, say, the perceptual and memory capacities of the injured person with those of people with intact brains. Of course, there are problems with this approach. Damage is not usually confined to a specific region.

Finding appropriate control subjects for comparison (i.e. people who are similar apart from not having brain injuries) also presents problems.

With animals it is possible to do precise experiments on the brain, though we can never afford to ignore the ethical questions that this raises. We can inject *marker* substances that have an affinity for certain classes of neuron. We can then examine the animal's brain under a microscope in order to trace out pathways. Again using animals, other techniques that are used to study the brain are electrical and chemical *stimulation* of specified brain regions through an implanted electrode or cannula. The assumption is commonly made that, by artificially stimulating the brain in this way, one is in some sense mimicking the natural activity of the region in question. A claim of this kind usually generates heated debate. It is argued that such stimulation, out of context, has abnormal effects.

Another possibility is to record electrically the activity of brain regions while the experimental subject behaves (it is assumed) naturally. Gross electrical activity of the brain can be recorded by electrodes attached to the head, a technique known as *electroencephalography* (EEG). In animals, recordings can also be made from individual cells in the brain by implanting electrodes. For example, Rolls (1975) has found neurons in the hypothalamus that are particularly responsive to the presentation of stimuli associated with food. Such cells show a particularly strong response to food-associated stimuli at times when the animal is food-deprived. Such observations, taken in the context of other investigations, lead Rolls to conclude that these neurons normally have a particular role to play in the motivational system (see Module 5) of feeding.

In recent years, the technique of monitoring *blood flow* in different brain regions has been developed. When a particular brain region is more active than usual—that is, a high rate of action potential generation by cells in the region—relatively large amounts of the fuels oxygen and glucose will be required by these cells. To supply these substances at a higher than normal rate, a local dilation of blood vessels in the region can sometimes be observed. This will bias blood flow towards the region. It is possible to detect such localized changes in blood flow by the use of special sensors attached to the scalp. When a human subject is asked, for example, to make a movement of the eyes or attend to a visual scene, an increase in blood flow can sometimes be seen at those regions concerned with vision and control of the eye muscles. What is even more interesting is that *mental processes*, such as mentally rehearsing a movement or counting silently, produce widespread alterations in blood flow in the brain.

SAQ 10
Describe four experimental approaches that can be used to investigate the function of a particular brain area.

Some insight into the role of brain mechanisms has been gained with the help of luck and accidental discovery. An example of this was the work in the early 1950s by James Olds on 'pleasure centres' in the brain (Olds, 1958). Olds observed what happened when an electrode, implanted in a region of the limbic system, was activated. If the electrode was activated when the rat was at a particular location in the room, the rat would tend to return to this location. It was as if the rat derived pleasure from such electrical stimulation. Furthermore, the rat would press a lever in a Skinner-box in order to administer shocks to this region of its own brain. Thus the region was implicated in motivation (see Module 5). The brain regions at which one could obtain such an effect came to be termed *pleasure centres*. Although the rat cannot, of course, report anything quite the same as the subjective state of pleasure in humans, the analogy is often irresistible. Humans who have experienced comparable stimulation do report pleasure or diminution of pain. Perhaps the word 'centre' should give even more cause for caution than the word 'pleasure'. If we are not careful, use of this word implies that pleasure is a property just of the brain region at the tip of the electrode. Rather, we should see the neuron(s) stimulated as playing a vital role in generation of the pleasure (or 'pleasure-like') state, but doing so in the context of other brain regions.

Perhaps due to its relative ease of access, the deeply-folded outer layer of the brain, the *cerebral cortex*, is one for which we have gained a particularly good understanding. Humans and other advanced mammals are characterized by an especially well-developed cerebral cortex. Another expression for cerebral cortex is *neocortex*. 'Neo' means 'new', and the expression refers to the fact that the cortex is a relatively recent evolutionary development. It is a much less prominent feature of the brains of reptiles than it is of mammals.

Parts of the cerebral cortex are concerned with the early stages of processing incoming sensory information. For example, an axon forming part of the optic nerve will (via an interconnecting neuron) make a connection with a cell in the cortex. Such a cell carries out further processing of visual information. Those parts of the cerebral cortex devoted to the receipt of sensory information entering the brain and the first stages of processing the incoming signals are together known as the *sensory cortex*. Sensory cortex is made up of regions concerned with processing visual information (visual cortex), auditory information (auditory cortex), information concerning smell (olfactory cortex) and information on touch (somatosensory cortex). Other regions of cortex are concerned with organizing the commands to the muscles and are known as *motor cortex*. Such regions having distinct functions are also anatomically distinct. Regions that have neither a clearly defined motor nor sensory function are defined, by exclusion, as 'non-specific' or *association cortex*.

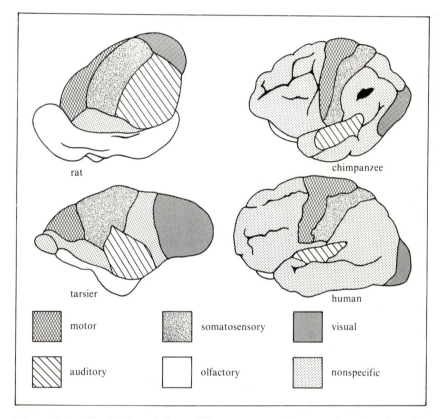

Figure 1.7   The brains of four different mammalian species, showing the divisions of the cortex. Note first the motor cortex in each case. Then inspect the sensory cortex. This is subdivided into the areas with which a particular sensory system is associated; that is, auditory, somatosensory (tactile sense), visual and olfactory (smell) regions. The remainder of cortex, not accounted for by such a sensory–motor classification, is defined as the non-specific, or 'association', cortex. Note how much larger a percentage of the human brain falls into this last category, as compared to the other species.

(Source: SD286 Module A.)

The functions of such regions is to associate (1) incoming sensory information after its first stages of processing in the sensory cortex and (2) motor commands.

Figure 1.7 shows the brains of four species. It can be seen that the association (non-specific) cortex occupies relatively more space in humans than in the other species. It is argued that this reflects the greater flexibility of human behaviour; that is, it is less tied to particular sensory inputs, and the behavioural choices are greater.

One of the best-known, and pioneering, studies on the neocortex was carried out by a neurosurgeon, Wilder Penfield. In the course of carrying out surgery on brain tissue, he tried electrically stimulating various regions of the cortex in conscious human subjects. Stimulation of certain regions of association cortex caused the subjects to recall particular memories, such as that of a piece of music or a conversation. Penfield was also able to map the motor cortex; electrical stimulation of a given location evoked a response in a given muscle. Stimulation of regions of visual cortex evoked the sensation of flashes of light, whereas stimulation of the auditory cortex was associated with the experience of auditory sensations.

It would be wrong to apply a simple interpretation to such results in terms of clearly defined discrete pathways and centres. However, tentatively, and with evidence derived by other means, we are able to plot some of the primary functions of different brain regions.

SAQ 11
The cerebral cortex can be divided into three different parts on the basis of general criteria of function served. What are these parts, and how do they differ?

Key Notes 1.6

1. Information about the role of various brain regions can be gained by electrical and chemical stimulation of various sites, lesions, monitoring of blood flow and recording the electrical activity of selected regions during 'normal' behaviour.
2. A picture can be built up of what regions have a particular role in what behaviour, and the way in which they process information. However, we must guard against naive assumptions of a simple one-to-one relationship between a given brain region and control of a given behaviour.
3. The cerebral cortex may be divided into sensory, motor and association regions.

Reading Guide

Blakemore, C. (1977) *Mechanics of the Mind*, Cambridge, Cambridge University Press.
Kalat, J.W. (1981) *Biological Psychology*, Belmont, Wadsworth.
Open University *SD286, Biology, Brain and Behaviour*, Module A,B3, Milton Keynes, Open University Educational Enterprises.

2 Neuron Module

Link from Introduction to the Neuron Module

In the last module we introduced the neuron, the basic unit or 'building block' of the nervous system. We described its function as a transmitter of information, in the form of a series of action potentials. We looked at the need for information to be transmitted by afferent and efferent neurons. The present module looks in more detail at the individual neuron and asks, amongst other things, what mechanism is involved in the initiation and transmission of an action potential.

General Diagnostic Questions for the Neuron Module

1. Under resting conditions, what are the factors determining the movement of sodium and potassium across the membrane of a neuron? (Sect. 2.1.)
2. Distinguish between the resting state of a neuron and the state when it is undergoing an action potential. (Sect. 2.2.)
3. How is information transmitted within a neuron and between neurons? (Sect. 2.3.)

2.1 The Resting Condition

Diagnostic Questions for Section 2.1

1. Describe what is meant by an 'ion'.
2. Describe an important difference in ion concentration between the inside and outside of a neuron.
3. Distinguish between a potential gradient and a concentration gradient.

Neurons carry information by means of the frequency with which they transmit action potentials. The action potential is a sudden impulse of electrical activity in the neuron. When the neuron is not conducting an action potential it is said to be in its 'resting' state. We normally start an account of the neuron by describing what is happening in this state.

Both the environment within the neuron (nerve cell) and that surrounding it consist, in large part, of substances dissolved in a solution of water. Therefore, imagine a fluid that permeates the inside of the cell, and another fluid of somewhat different composition permeating the outside (see Fig. 2.1). A *membrane* separates the two fluids, forming a boundary between them. Each fluid contains particles of different substances. The fluid inside the cell is rich in potassium but has relatively little sodium. Conversely, the fluid outside the cell is rich in sodium but has a low concentration of potassium. Sodium and potassium are examples of what are known as 'ions'.

To understand the term *ion*, a short digression is necessary. Consider the substance sodium chloride, common table-salt, a compound composed of the constituents sodium and chloride ions. If a quantity of sodium chloride is dissolved in water, each of the many molecules of sodium chloride breaks down into its two constituents. Each constituent then carries a small 'package' of electricity, known as a *charge*. A particle carrying such a charge is known as an 'ion'. Sodium (symbol: Na) carries one kind of electrical charge, termed 'positive', and therefore a sodium ion is indicated as Na^+. Chloride (Cl) carries a charge of opposite properties to a positive ion and is known as a 'negative' charge. Hence, the chloride ion is represented as Cl^-. (Potassium, whose chemical symbol is K, carries a positive charge, and is designated as K^+.)

To summarize, by dissolving a quantity of sodium chloride in water, we obtain a solution containing a number of positive sodium ions and a number of negative chloride ions. Sodium and chloride are just two of the many types of ion that are found in large numbers in all living systems, and play a vital role in their functioning.

So far we have described the situation that prevails on the inside and outside of the cell: different concentrations of various substances. We now move to consider the consequences of such a distribution. In a situation where there is a higher concentration of a *particular* substance in one location than in another, a *concentration gradient* for that substance is said to exist. All other things being equal, this gradient creates a tendency for particles of the substance to move down the gradient; that is, to move from the region of high concentration to that of low concentration. (Such a tendency exists whether or not the substance carries an electric charge.) For example, in Figure 2.1 the potassium concentration gradient tends to move potassium particles from the inside of the cell to the outside.

SAQ 12
With reference to Figure 2.1, what is the tendency created by the sodium concentration gradient?

So much for the tendency created by the existence of concentration gradients. We now need to consider the additional consequence of the *electrical* properties of the substances described.

'Like' ions (i.e. two positive ions or two negative ions) repel each other. 'Unlike' ions, a positive and a negative, attract each other. If there is an equal number of positive and negative ions in a region, the charges cancel out and electrical neutrality is said to result.

Consider an individual nerve cell. Suppose there is an imbalance of ions on the inside of the cell, let us say an excess of positive ions.

SAQ 13
The word 'excess' as used here is with reference to what?

Outside the cell there is a balance of positive and negative ions. The imbalance inside the cell will create a force tending to move positive ions out of the cell. The same force will tend to pull negative ions into the cell. Let us call such a force a 'positive voltage'. Now consider the opposite imbalance: an excess of *negative* ions on the inside. This will tend to move negative ions out of the cell and pull positive ions in. Such a force is termed a 'negative voltage'.

By the use of a voltmeter, we can measure the existence of such an electrical voltage between the inside and the outside of the neuron (i.e. across the membrane), which is known as the *membrane potential*.

Under 'resting conditions' (i.e. when no action potential is occurring) the inside of the nerve cell is electrically negative with respect to the outside. The *resting potential*, the electrical state of the cell when not exhibiting an action potential, is usually around -70 millivolts (mV). That is to say, the cell has a net surplus of negative ions.

The existence of a membrane potential means that a force exists that is able to move ions across the membrane. When we speak of *movement*, we refer to the electrical potential across the membrane as a *potential gradient*. This then gives us a common 'currency' for considering the two forces that act to move ions across the membrane: the concentration gradient and potential gradient. (Actually, only a very tiny percentage of the total ion population need move in order to create a very large change in the potential). Hence, the inside of the cell being electrically negative will attract positive ions such as sodium (down the potential gradient).

SAQ 14
What is the influence of the potential gradient in so far as negative ions are concerned?

You should note one difference between the two types of gradient discussed so far. The concentration gradient is defined in terms of a specific substance; for example, the sodium concentration gradient or the potassium concentration gradient. The potential gradient depends upon the total ion population on either side of the membrane; that is, the imbalance in ions. This is regardless of the particular substances that contribute to this imbalance. Thus, as far as the potential gradient is concerned, a deficiency of a negative ion (e.g. chloride, in one place will have the same effect as an excess of a positive ion (e.g. sodium) in the same place.

To summarize, both concentration and potential gradients cause the movement of ions. The concentration gradient depends upon concentration differences specific to the ion type in question. The potential gradient depends upon the effect of all ion types present. The net effect upon a given type of ion depends upon the combined influences of the concentration gradient and the potential gradient. These can act in the same or opposite directions depending upon the particular ion in question and the distribution of other ions.

SAQ 15
What is the influence of the potassium concentration gradient and potential gradient in so far as the movement of potassium is concerned?

Both the sodium concentration gradient and the potential gradient are in the direction to move sodium into the cell. What then is the combined effect of these two gradients in moving Na^+? Movement of ions across the membrane depends not only upon the gradients present but also upon the permeability properties of the membrane itself, known as 'membrane permeability'. Under resting conditions the membrane is relatively impermeable to sodium; that is, the resistance to Na^+ movement across the membrane is high. Nonetheless, there is a small trickle of sodium into the cell under the combined influence of the two gradients.

A *sodium pump* forces sodium out at a rate equal to that at which

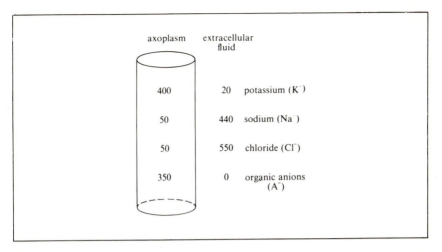

Figure 2.1   The relative concentration of some of the major ions on the inside (axoplasm) and outside (extracellular fluid) of the neuron. The neuron is represented as a cylinder, containing fluid (axoplasm). The wall of the cylinder is the membrane that surrounds the cell. This membrane separates the axoplasm from the fluid on the outside.
(Source: SD286 Module B1.)

it enters, so the concentration remains very close to that shown in Figure 2.1. The sodium pump is an essential feature of the living organism. Life depends upon maintaining concentrations of ions very close to those shown in this figure, and so the inherent tendency for this segregation to break down needs correction.

Key Notes 2.1

1. The inside of the neuron is rich in potassium but has a relatively low sodium concentration. The opposite is true of the fluid outside the cell.
2. A concentration gradient exists where a particular substance is unequally distributed between the inside and outside of a cell.
3. A potential gradient exists where there is an uneven distribution of the total number of positive and negative charged particles (ions).
4. The tendency of any ion to move depends upon the *net* effect of the concentration gradient for that particular ion type (e.g. sodium) and the potential gradient.
5. The tendency for an ion type to move across the membrane

depends also upon the permeability that the membrane exhibits to that particular ion type.

6. Under resting conditions, in spite of the combined effect of two gradients tending to move sodium into the cell, only a trickle enters because membrane permeability to sodium is low.

7. Over a period of time, a sodium pump moves sodium out of the cell at a rate equal to that at which it enters down the concentration and potential gradients.

2.2   Basis of the Action Potential

Diagnostic Questions for Section 2.2

1. Describe the shape of the action potential.
2. Relate the sequence of events observed in the action potential to changes in membrane permeability and movement of ions across the membrane.

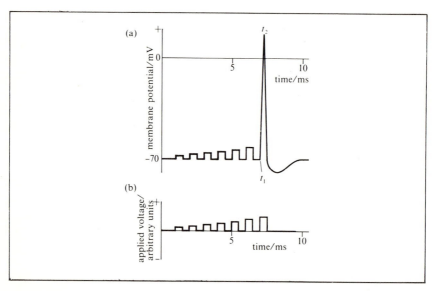

Figure 2.2   The effect of applying an artificial voltage in increasing steps of magnitude to the neuron. (a) Membrane potential. (b) Stimulus voltage. Note the resting potential of the membrane at about -70 mV, and the step displacements caused by application of the stimulus. At time t_1, the membrane shows a sudden large depolarization. At time t_2, repolarization is initiated.

(Source: SD286 Module B1.)

As pointed out in the previous section, in its resting condition, the membrane of the neuron has a relatively low permeability to sodium. However, a feature that characterizes the neuron is that it can change its membrane permeability. For the sake of simplification in explaining how this can arise, suppose that we are able to stimulate the neuron with an artificial electrical voltage. By these means we create a small and temporary change in the electrical potential across the membrane of the neuron. An example of such artificial stimulation and its effect is shown in Figure 2.2. To the far left of Figure 2.2b we see the first applied stimulus (a very small step change in voltage), and, immediately above it (Fig. 2.2a), the resultant change in membrane potential. As we apply a small positive voltage, so we obtain a small change in membrane potential in a positive direction.

The key characteristic of the neuron is that the *permeability* of the membrane to sodium depends upon *membrane potential*. As the membrane potential is made less negative (i.e. it moves in a positive direction), so the membrane becomes more permeable to sodium. In response to the applied stimulus, not only would membrane potential change slightly (as shown in Fig. 2.2a) but also there would be a slight transient increase in membrane sodium permeability.

SAQ 16
Which factors determine the rate at which sodium enters the neuron?

As a result of the increase in membrane sodium permeability, a slight increase in the rate of movement of sodium into the cell would result (relative to the undisturbed resting condition).

As shown in Figure 2.2b, we then proceed, in a series of steps, to increase the magnitude of the applied stimulation. Up to a point, for each increase, there is a commensurate change in the membrane potential (Fig. 2.2a). However, at time t_1, we reach a *threshold*. For only a slight further increase in the magnitude of the applied stimulus, there is a dramatic effect. Under the influence of both the sodium concentration gradient and the potential gradient, sodium enters the cell in relatively large amounts. This influx of positively charged ions changes the membrane potential. Membrane potential rapidly swings upwards towards zero, overshoots to a positive value (time t_2), and then abruptly swings back to the region of the resting potential (-70 mV). This abrupt change in the electrical state of the cell is known as the *action potential*. A move of membrane potential away from the resting potential in a positive direction is known as *depolarization*. Its return to the resting potential is known as *repolarization*.

The basis of the action potential lies, to a considerable extent, in abrupt changes in membrane permeability to sodium and potassium. Up to time t_1, each increase in the size of the applied stimulus causes a corresponding transient increase in sodium permeability. At time t_2, a radical change occurs. The neuron gets into a state that we might describe as a 'vicious circle', or, if you prefer a different analogy, 'the system picks itself up by its own bootstraps'. At t_1, the inflow of sodium reaches a point where sodium permeability increases abruptly. This increases the inflow of sodium, which makes the potential less negative, which increases sodium permeability, which increases sodium inflow, and so on. This is truly a self-reinforcing set of interactions, and hence the dramatic shift to a positive value of membrane potential.

How is it that the swing in membrane potential stops at a particular positive value? To answer this we need to look more closely at the membrane. Sodium and potassium are able to pass across the membrane via specific *channels*, and passage of ions through these channels is regulated by *gates*. Thus we speak of, for example, the 'sodium channel' and the 'potassium channel' through which sodium and potassium respectively are able to pass the membrane. The gates can swing open or shut, as if on hinges. The degree of opening of these gates determines how permeable the membrane channel is to the ion in question. As the membrane potential moves from its resting value in a positive direction, so the sodium gates become relatively open.

These channels are distinct from the routes through which the sodium pump moves sodium ions across the membrane. This process of active sodium pumping goes on at a relatively steady rate against the background of opening and closing of sodium channels.

SAQ 17
Low sodium permeability would be associated with what condition of the gates in the membrane?

The characteristics of the sodium channels change markedly at the onset of the action potential. The gates open relatively widely to allow sodium through. However, immediately after opening, the sodium gates close again. This explains how the inward rush of sodium is halted, and consequently why the move of membrane potential in a positive direction is halted.

What then is the mechanism that underlies the move of membrane potential in a *negative* direction at time t_2, towards the resting potential (repolarization)? The mechanism is as follows. Just as sodium is able to cross the membrane through sodium channels, so are there specific potassium channels, through which potassium is able to cross. For either ion to cross, not only must the gates to the channels be open, but there must exist a force to move it across. The gates controlling these potassium channels are able to change their opening, according to circumstances. At time t_2, although the permeability to sodium is very low, that shown towards potassium is relatively high. Therefore potassium moves *out* of the cell, down its concentration gradient. This movement of positive charge out of the cell moves the membrane potential towards its resting potential (around -70 mV).

SAQ 18
The concentration gradient for potassium will cause a movement of potassium out of the cell. At time t_2 and after, what will be the effect of the *potential gradient* in so far as the movement of potassium (a positive ion) is concerned?

SAQ 19
Figure 2.3 shows the effect of applying a stimulus that (at time 2) slowly moves membrane potential away from its resting value (depolarizes). Give an account of the changes in membrane permeability and ion flows at the various times indicated (1–7) in Figure 2.3; that is, before, during and after application of the depolarizing stimulus.

After the membrane has undergone the series of changes just described—that is, the action potential—for a few milliseconds it is unable to repeat the sequence. It is unresponsive ('refractory') to stimulation, and this period is known as the *refractory period*.

So far in this module, to simplify the explanation, we have discussed the action potential as something occurring at a particular location in the neuron. This is not incorrect; if we stimulate appropriately a part of a neuron, the particular region stimulated will undergo the sequence of events termed the action potential. However, we noted in Module 1 that action potentials are the means by which information can be transmitted over relatively large distances. For example, an action potential caused by tissue damage might arise at one end of a neuron (e.g. the skin) and be transmitted along the length of the neuron to the spinal cord. How can an action potential at one end of a neuron give rise to changes in the neuron

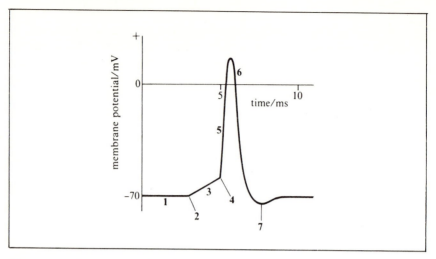

Figure 2.3 The effect of applying a gradual depolarizing stimulus at time 2.
(Source: SD286, Module B1.)

such that the action potential is transmitted along the length of the cell?

An action potential arising at one location will cause depolarization of a neighbouring region of the same neuron. In response to such depolarization, this newly stimulated region will then also undergo the sequence of changes characterizing the action potential. In turn, it will stimulate the next neighbouring region. In effect, the action potential moves along the neuron from the point of stimulation to the point most distant. Although the region to both sides of that undergoing the action potential will be stimulated, the action potential moves in one direction only. Figure 2.4 illustrates this. The action potential moves into a region that has not recently been stimulated. It does not travel backwards, since there is a refractory period and a section of neuron just stimulated will be refractory to further stimulation.

Analogies for understanding the action potential abound: it is rather like a spark travelling along a fuse-wire; the heat in one region will ignite the next region, and so on. If you prefer mechanical analogies, a falling row of dominoes might help. Psychologists might like to compare the process with the phi-phenomenon, by which the lights at Piccadilly Circus appear to move sideways. One light extinguishes as another is illuminated, and the bulb itself appears to be moving. In the action potential, one region undergoes the change,

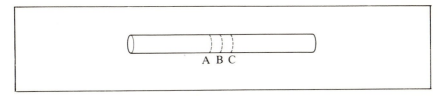

Figure 2.4   Sketch of part of a neuron that is transmitting an action potential. Let us say that at the time in question the action potential has reached point B. It is travelling from left to right. It will therefore have just passed point A. The existence of an action potential at point B will create conditions within a short distance to either side of B that will tend to generate another action potential. However, the part of the cell in region A has just undergone the sequence of changes that characterize the action potential. This means that a new action potential cannot arise there until a period of time, the 'refractory period', has elapsed. C is able to undergo the sequence of changes called the action potential. Hence the action potential in effect moves from A to B to C, from left to right along the length of the cell. By the time each region passed has recovered sufficiently to undergo another action potential, the original one will have moved too far away for a new one to arise. Hence an indefinite reverberation does not occur.

which induces the change in the neighbouring region. For most purposes, it is easiest to say that the action potential moves along the axon.

Key Notes 2.2

1. When an increase in membrane permeability to sodium exceeds a certain threshold, an abrupt shift of the membrane potential in a positive direction occurs (depolarization).
2. The increased flow of sodium into the cell and move of membrane potential in a positive direction terminate when the sodium channels close.
3. Closure of sodium channels is accompanied by opening of potassium channels and a movement of potassium out of the cell. This restores membrane potential to its negative resting potential.
4. Following one action potential, the nerve cell is refractory to further stimulation for a few milliseconds.
5. An action potential can travel along a neuron from the site where it arises to a distant site. This is the basis of information transmission by action potentials.

2.3   The Classical Neuron

Diagnostic Questions for Section 2.3

1. Describe the sequence of events that might arise following the arrival of a series of action potentials simultaneously at a number of excitatory synapses.
2. Explain, in terms of the synaptic input to a neuron, how excitation and inhibition are produced.
3. In what way can a neuron perform a simple calculation?
4. What is the significance of the fact that there is more than one type of transmitter substance?
5. What is meant by a 'dopaminergic neuron'?

For simplification, up to now we have sometimes spoken rather loosely of *the* neuron, as if there were just one type, having a uniform shape. In fact, neurons come in a variety of shapes and sizes, and function in a variety of different ways. However, the focus for explanation of the action potential is usually upon what we might call the 'textbook' or 'classical' neuron, shown in Figure 2.5. An important feature of this type of neuron is a *cell body* or *soma*. There is a major extension running from the soma, termed the *axon*. Other processes also develop out from the soma, these being the *dendrites*.

Suppose action potentials are carried over a particular distance, called *x*. For example, we might think of the transmission of action potentials from the foot to the brain. Such action potentials could inform us that we are standing on a wet or hot object. Over the distance *x*, the information will be transmitted by a series of neurons. This means that one neuron must be able to make contact with another, so that an action potential in one can instigate an action potential in another.

The point at which one nerve cell influences another is known as a *synapse*. At the type of synapse that we shall now consider, two neurons almost fuse together. However, on close microscopic examination there can be seen to be a small gap between them. In Figure 2.5, consider the three cells to the left that *synapse* upon the dendrites of the classical neuron (e.g. that communicating at synapse 1). These three cells convey inputs to the classical neuron; by their electrical activity they are able to change its electrical condition. For example, activity in these three inputs might have an *excitatory* (i.e. depolarizing) effect; that is, their activity would increase the probability of the cell generating an action potential. Action potentials in the classical neuron arise at a point on the axon known as the *axon hillock*, indicated by the dotted line. They then travel away from the

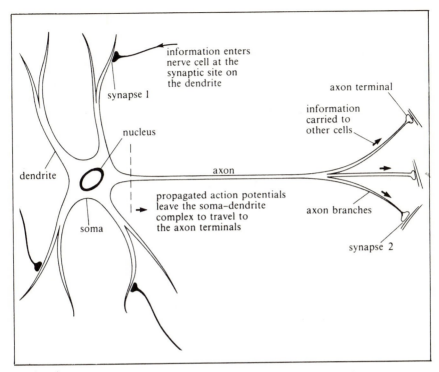

Figure 2.5   The classical neuron, consisting of a soma, axon and dendrites. For full explanation see text.

(Source SD286: Module B1.)

soma along the axon. Note that, in this particular example, the 'parent' axon gives rise to three terminal branches. What was previously one action potential becomes, after the branching, three action potentials, travelling in the three branches. At each *axon terminal* the neuron forms a synapse with another neuron (e.g. synapse 2).

SAQ 20

Suppose that the input impinging on the classical neuron at a large number of synapses is sufficiently excitatory to generate an action potential. Is there any limit on how frequently action potentials can arise at the axon hillock and be transmitted along the axon?

Let us now consider more closely the sequence of events at a synapse that transfers information from one neuron *to* the classical neuron of Figure 2.5 (e.g. at synapse 1). An action potential arrives at the axon terminal of one of the neurons providing input to the classical neuron (e.g. that forming part of synapse 1). On arriving at the axon terminal, the action potential causes the release of a chemical *transmitter* substance (e.g. acetylcholine or dopamine). Synapse 1 and the other synapses that are described in this module are known as *chemical synapses* because they employ a chemical as the agent of transmission. Prior to its release, the transmitter substance is held at the axon terminal at synapse 1. Following its release, the transmitter rapidly migrates across the synaptic gap and attaches itself to *receptors* in the membrane on the other side (in this case, the membrane of a dendrite). This process can be compared to a key (a specific transmitter substance) fitting a lock (a specific receptor site). To develop the analogy, in the nervous system there are many different 'keys', each of which can fit one of the various 'locks' on neuronal cell membranes.

The permeability of the membrane to ions is changed by the process of the attachment of transmitter to receptors; for example, a particular transmitter, on finding its specific receptor, might increase the permeability of the membrane to sodium. Considering a single synapse, the arrival of excitatory transmitter would have a slight depolarizing effect that would extend to the axon hillock. In such a cell, a single synaptic input would normally be insufficient to make a significant difference as far as the generation of action potentials is concerned. However, if a number of excitatory inputs are simultaneously activated (e.g. the two shown in addition to synapse 1, and others not shown) then the combined effect might be enough to cause a significant depolarization at the axon hillock. A series of action potentials might then be provoked and would, in turn, travel along the axon to the far end of the neuron.

So much for the input *to* our classical neuron and the possible generation of an action potential. Let us now turn our attention to the cell's output. Action potentials generated at the axon hillock travel to the axon terminals of our classical neuron, shown to the right of Figure 2.5. (Take care not to confuse these axon terminals with those of the cells that impinge upon the classical neuron, e.g. at synapse 1). On arrival, action potentials cause the release of transmitter substance stored at the terminal. The transmitter migrates across the synaptic gap and influences the electrical state of other nerve cells, small bits of which (sections of dendrite) are shown on the far right of the figure.

So far, we have spoken of the neuron as something serving the role of a transmitter of signals over a certain distance. This is indeed an important role served by neurons, but now we need to look at their other roles, such as the ability to perform computation. Before doing this, it will be useful to define the terms *presynaptic* and *postsynaptic*. With respect to a given synapse, the presynaptic cell is that which releases the transmitter. The postsynaptic cell is that which is influenced by the transmitter. Synapses can be excitatory, as we have just described. This means that electrical activity in the presynaptic cell depolarizes the postsynaptic cell. However, synapses can also be *inhibitory*; that is to say, activity in the presynaptic cell inhibits the generation of action potentials in the postsynaptic cell. Whether a particular synapse is excitatory or inhibitory depends upon the type of transmitter substance that is used and the nature of the receptor mechanism to which it attaches itself at the postsynaptic membrane.

SAQ 21
Suppose that a particular neuron has a number of excitatory synapses (A, B, C ...) bringing information to the cell. It also has a number of inhibitory synapses (1, 2, 3 ...) bringing information. What distribution of activity in the presynaptic cells would maximize the chances of the generation of action potentials in the postsynaptic cell?

Activity in a neuron might therefore signify that there is activity in some of its presynaptic cells but not in others. This introduces a simple example of the *computation* ability of a neuron; its activity level is a measure of the relative weightings of input at its excitatory and inhibitory synapses. A strong activity level would indicate a dominant excitatory input, whereas no activity could mean a dominant inhibitory input.

SAQ 22
What do we mean by the 'activity level' of a neuron? What does it mean to say that a neuron is 'strongly excited'.

Figure 2.6 shows an enlarged view of a synapse between two neurons, in this case a so-called *axo-dendritic* synapse. This expression means that the axon of one cell (presynaptic) makes a synapse upon the dendrite of another cell (postsynaptic). Other possible combinations of parts of neurons forming a synapse exist. Note the *vesicles* that hold the transmitter substance prior to its release into the gap between the two membranes, known as the *synaptic cleft*, on the arrival of an action potential at the terminal of neuron 1.

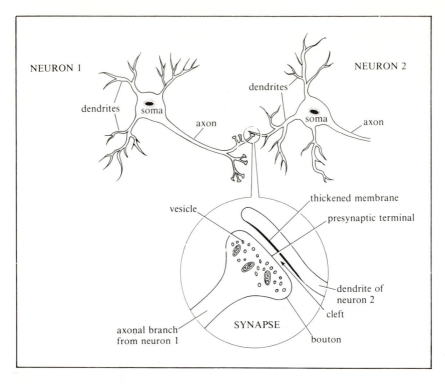

Figure 2.6 Two neurons in interaction. Neuron 1 influences neuron 2 at an axo-dendritic synapse, shown enlarged. Note the axonal branch from neuron 1, swelling into a bouton. Chemical transmitter substance is held in *vesicles* prior to its release from the presynaptic membrane. Note also the gap, or *cleft*, between the two cells, across which the transmitter migrates following its release. Transmitter then impinges upon the membrane of a dendrite of neuron 2, the postsynaptic membrane.
(Source: SD286 Module B1.)

SAQ 23
In figure 2.5, does the classical neuron provide the presynaptic or the postsynaptic membrane?

Looking at neurons in different parts of the brain, we find a rich variety of chemicals that can serve the role of transmitter. Two such substances are dopamine and acetylcholine. Whether a given synapse is excitatory or inhibitory depends upon both the transmitter substance employed at the synapse and the postsynaptic membrane. It is the mode of interaction of the transmitter with receptors at the postsynaptic membrane that determines whether the influence is excitatory or inhibitory. Transmitter substance is synthesized within a cell and stored at the terminal. For some purposes a cell is defined by the transmitter that it releases; for example, a dopaminergic cell is one that synthesizes and releases dopamine. Turning to the input side, more than one transmitter can influence a given cell at its various synaptic inputs; for example, one substance might excite the cell at one synapse, whereas at another synapse a different substance might inhibit the cell.

Key Notes 2.3

1. The 'classical' neuron that is traditionally described is one in which a number of synapses impinge upon dendrites. Action potentials can arise at the axon hillock and travel along the axon.
2. Most synapses employ a chemical transmitter substance. A cell releases transmitter at a presynaptic terminal. This transmitter migrates across the synaptic cleft, and influences the post-synaptic membrane (i.e. part of another cell).
3. Transmitters may either excite, making an action potential in the postsynaptic cell more likely, or inhibit, making it less likely.
4. The neuron is able to perform computation upon incoming excitatory and inhibitory information.
5. For some purposes, a cell can be characterized by the species of transmitter that it synthesizes, stores and releases.

Reading Guide

Bloom, F. E., Lazerson, A. and Hofstader, L. (1985) *Brain, Mind and Behaviour*, New York, W. H. Freeman.

Kandel, E. R. and Schwartz, J. H. (1983) *Principles of Neural Science*, London, E. Arnold.

Kuffler, S. W. and Nicholls, J. G. (1977) *From Neuron to Brain*, Sunderland, Sinauer.

Open University *SD286, Biology, Brain and Behaviour*, Module B1, Milton Keynes, Open University Educational Enterprises.

3 Neuronal Systems Module

Link from the Neuron Module to Neuronal Systems Module

In the last module we described some of the characteristics of neurons, such as their internal environment and membrane. We then looked at a particular type of neuron that we termed the 'classical neuron'. In this module we shall look at how neurons form systems and how an understanding of the characteristics of individual cells is vital in understanding the properties of a system made up of such cells. We shall also gain some impression of the rich variety of different neurons that exist. Some of these neither look like the classical neuron nor exhibit action potentials. First, we consider a relatively simple nervous system, that of the sea slug *Aplysia*. We show how an understanding of neuronal properties can beautifully illustrate the bases of a simple behaviour. The following two sections, on the visual system and on pain, look at neuronal systems in more advanced animals. In each case it is argued that by looking at simplified *features* of complex systems we can gain considerable insight. For the two examples chosen, we are able to understand rather well how neurons connected together to form particular systems can explain features of phenomena at a behavioural level. However, it will be emphasized that at present we can do no more than to explain certain features or 'aspects' of behaviour in terms of neuronal circuits.

General Diagnostic Questions for Neuronal Systems

1. In relation to the gill-retraction reflex of *Aplysia*, explain what is meant by the terms habituation, dishabituation, sensitization and spontaneous recovery. (Sect. 3.1)
2. Show where a knowledge of neuronal interactions can help to explain how the visual system is particularly sensitive to contours. (Sect. 3.2)
3. Why might it be misleading to employ the term 'pain receptor' to describe a nociceptor? (Sect. 3.3.)

3.1 Gill-Retraction Reflex of Aplysia

Diagnostic Questions for Section 3.1

1. What is the consequence for the motor neuron of a decrease in the amount of transmitter released by the sensory neuron?

2. What is the role of calcium channels in the habituation and dishabituation of the gill-retraction reflex of *Aplysia*.
3. In terms of the function that it serves, how might one explain the gill-retraction reflex, as well as its habituation and dishabituation.

Using the giant sea slug *Aplysia*, Eric Kandel and associates (Kandel and Schwartz, 1982) have been able to identify the cellular bases of a behavioural phenomenon, known as habituation, in the animal's nervous system. The advantage of using such a species is that its nervous system is relatively simple, made up of relatively few neurons. Furthermore, these neurons are much larger than those normally found in more complex animals, hence facilitating recording from identified individual nerve cells.

Figure 3.1 shows a diagram of an *Aplysia*. On the left the animal is in its undisturbed state, and, as can be seen, the gill is exposed. On the right, the animal is shown after the siphon has been touched by a tactile stimulus. The gill, a vitally important but delicate respiratory organ, has retracted in response to the tactile stimulus. This is a defence mechanism which serves to protect the gill from, for example, being bitten off by a predator. Suppose we repeatedly stimulate the siphon, and see what happens to the gill response.

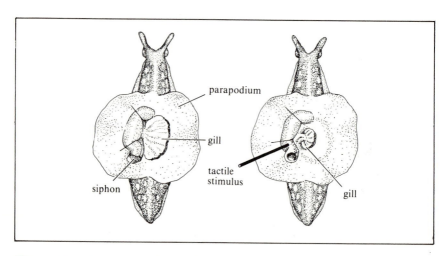

Figure 3.1 The marine slug *Aplysia*. (a) In its undisturbed condition, with the gill relatively exposed. (b) After a tactile stimulus has been applied to the siphon, showing the gill in a relatively retracted state.
(Source: SD286, Module B2.)

Techniques Box B

Observing a Response

Figure 3.2 shows an experimental set-up that is used by Kandel and associates for measuring the gill-retraction response of *Aplysia*. The animal is constrained in a small aquarium. The siphon is stimulated with a jet of water (the water pik). The extent of gill retraction is measured by a photocell. The more the gill retracts the more light that falls onto the photocell. Hence, one can calibrate the output of the photocell in terms of the magnitude of gill retraction. The left section of Figure 3.3 shows what happens when the gill-retraction reflex is stimulated ten times in a period of 8 minutes. The value of 100 per cent is given to the magnitude of the contraction that occurs on first presentation of the stimulus. The time at which this is presented is designated as time 0.

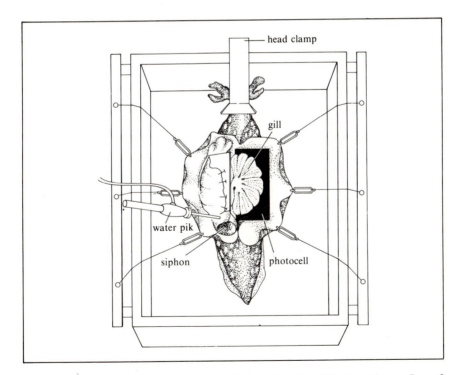

Figure 3.2   Experimental apparatus for testing the gill-retraction reflex of *Aplysia*.
(Source: SD286, Module B2.)

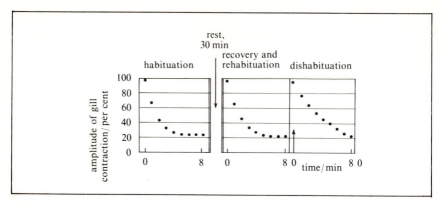

Figure 3.3 Habituation, spontaneous recovery and dishabituation in *Aplysia*. At first, repeated presentation of a stimulus results in a decrement in the strength of the response evoked, known as *habituation*. Following a 30-minute rest period, presentation of the same stimulus evokes a more powerful response, a process known as *spontaneous recovery*. A second session of repeated presentation of the same stimulus causes the reappearance of habituation, known as *rehabituation*. Suppose a powerful stimulus (B) is then applied to, say, the head (indicated by the arrow pointing vertically upwards). Presentation of the *original* tactile stimulus either immediately (as here), or some time after such a strong stimulus, causes a powerful gill-retraction response. This process is termed *dishabituation*.

SAQ 24

How would you describe the result of repeatedly stimulating over an 8-minute period?

This phenomenon is known as *habituation*. How might we explain this behaviour in terms of the advantage that it confers upon the animal? There is little point in the animal responding unless some benefit is to be gained by so doing. Since the same tactile stimulation of the siphon had been repeated eight times with no harmful effect, there is no imperative for the animal to take action. Expressed in other words, it had learnt that it could afford not to respond; the particular stimulus had been shown to be innocuous. In Figure 3.3, note what happens when a rest period of 30 minutes is allowed, and then the same stimulus is again applied. The response recovers its full strength. Such recovery in strength, which is revealed when the animal is stimulated following a rest period, is known as *spontaneous recovery*. The term is a slight misnomer; even though the recovery process itself might be called spontaneous, it is only revealed by stimulating the *Aplysia*.

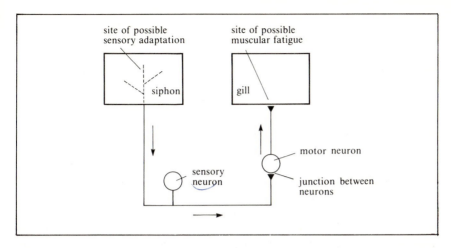

Figure 3.4   The two neurons of *Aplysia* that are implicated in habituation.
A decrease in the magnitude of the response might be due to changes at any
of several sites. There might be sensory adaptation, which would place the
change at the sensory end; relatively little electrical activity would be evoked
by a given stimulus after repeated presentation. Conversely, the decrease in
responsiveness could be at the motor output end (e.g. muscular fatigue).
Experimentation has however shown that the change is central; it is located
within the sensory–motor synapse.
(Source: SD286, Module B2.)

Examine Figure 3.4. This shows the two neurons that are implicated in the gill-retraction reflex in *Aplysia*. A sensory neuron runs
from the siphon and forms a synapse with a motor neuron. (Note
that this sensory neuron looks very different to the classical neuron
described in Module 2). The motor neuron then influences a muscle
of the gill. Simply from the behavioural observations shown in
Figure 3.3, we would not know at what site in this neuronal system
the changes underlying habituation are to be found. In principle, it
could be at the sensory or motor ends or somewhere between.
However, careful investigations by Kandel and associates have
located the synapse between sensory and motor neurons as the site
of the physical change forming the basis of habituation (described
below).

SAQ 25
What is the effect of the arrival of an action potential at a synapse
that employs a chemical transmitter substance?

For *Aplysia*, as the stimulus to the siphon is repeated several times in succession, on each occasion less transmitter substance is released from the sensory neuron. This shows that the change underlying habituation occurs *before* the synaptic gap between sensory and motor neurons. But where exactly does it occur? It is possible to stimulate the sensory neuron artificially and thereby to make sure that the signal in the sensory neuron is constant over a series of trials. Using this procedure, one can see that successive action potentials in the sensory neuron cause less and less transmitter to be released. This mimics natural habituation, and hence a change at the presynaptic site is implicated as the physical basis of habituation.

To understand the basis of habituation, it is necessary to consider more closely events in the sensory neuron. The ion calcium is present in the extracellular fluid that bathes the neuron. Calcium plays a crucial role in the process of releasing the chemical transmitter from the sensory neuron. Arrival of an action potential at the presynaptic membrane causes calcium to enter through calcium channels in the membrane. This calcium entry stimulates release of the chemical transmitter from the terminal of the sensory neuron. Kandel has established that the cellular basis of habituation is a closure of these calcium channels. This means that the arrival of an action potential in the habituated system is associated with a relatively low influx of calcium and a correspondingly low release of transmitter substance.

SAQ 26
Look back to Figure 3.3 (p. 46). Following the rest period and spontaneous recovery, what is the effect of repeating the series of stimuli?

When the system is habituated, a disturbance of some significance, such as a tactile stimulus to the head (let's call it B) *sensitizes* the system. If the *original* test stimulus of siphon stimulation (A) is applied just after such an extraneous stimulus (B) is given, the response to the original stimulus (A) is restored. This phenomenon is termed *dishabituation* and is illustrated in Figure 3.3. In this case, full recovery of the response is evident for a siphon stimulus (A) applied immediately after the stimulus (B) was applied to the head. After this dishabituation, repetition of the siphon stimulus (A) leads again to habituation, as shown in Figure 3.3.

SAQ 27
Distinguish between spontaneous recovery and dishabituation.

What advantage might dishabituation confer upon the animal? A strong novel tactile stimulus to the head could spell general danger.

It might signal a predator or very rough weather. Any subsequent stimulation of the siphon could similarly reflect danger, and so increased responsiveness to such a stimulus would be in order. The habituated system would have been, in a sense, 'lulled into security'. The new conditions counter this.

In the habituated system the calcium channels in the terminal portion of the sensory neuron are relatively closed, and hence little transmitter is released by the arrival of an action potential. The behaviour of dishabituation might therefore be expected to be associated with a reversal of this state: an opening of the calcium channels, termed *sensitization*. Kandel and associates have obtained evidence to suggest that this is indeed the case. Figure 3.5 shows how such sensitization appears to occur. A neuron, marked 'interneuron' influences the sensory–motor synapse. This interneuron releases the chemical transmitter *serotonin*, which opens up calcium channels. Stimulation of the head (e.g. by sharp tap) activates the interneuron, causing release of serotonin. This opens calcium channels, sensitizing the system. When the siphon is restimulated a larger amount of transmitter is released in the sensitized system, and hence the response is larger.

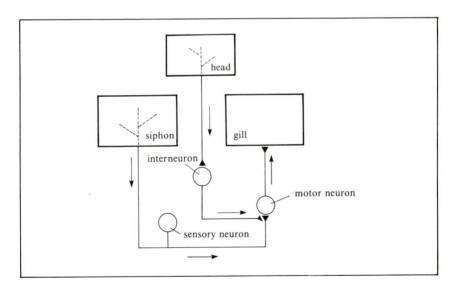

Figure 3.5 Neural model of the system underlying habituation and dishabituation. The sensitivity of the synapse between the sensory and motor neurons determines how responsive the system is to stimulation. This sensitivity can be changed by activity in the interneuron.
(Source: SD286, Module B2.)

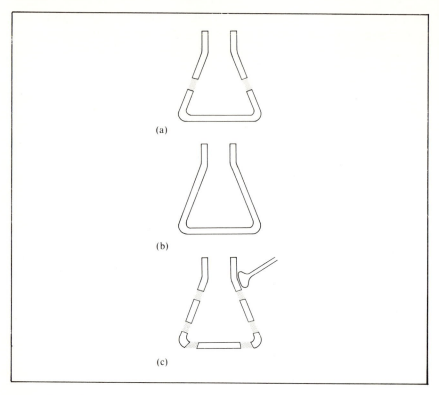

Figure 3.6 Representation of the terminal of the sensory neuron. (a) Normal condition, showing some calcium channels open. (b) Habituated system, showing closure of channels. (c) Sensitized system, showing channels open to greater extent than normal. In (c), note the terminal of the interneuron synapsing with the terminal of the sensory neuron.
(Source: SD286, Module C2.)

Figure 3.6 shows the terminal of the sensory neuron including its calcium channels. Figure 3.6b shows the habituated system with calcium channels closed, and Figure 3.6c shows the state of the membrane following sensitization by the interneuron.

SAQ 28
In what way does the sensitized system shown in Figure 3.6c differ from the system prior to habituation, as shown in Figure 3.6a?

Sensitization by the interneuron can be such that an habituated system is restored to its full pre-habituation strength. However, as Figure 3.6 suggests, the effect of sensitization can sometimes be even stronger than this, so that the response increases to above its unsensitized value.

SAQ 29
Examine Figure 3.3. In this particular case, is the degree of sensitization such that the response post-sensitization is even greater than before habituation was started?

The results of Kandel and his associates are in many ways an example of neurobiology at its best. A behavioural phenomenon has been clearly associated with its cellular bases. Kandel refers to the changes at the habituated synapse as being a kind of memory of the past events. A stimulus is repeated with no harmful consequence to the animal, and this series of events is coded in an identifiable change in the nervous system. To what extent this model, based upon a relatively simple nervous system, will prove useful in the study of more complex nervous systems will be shown with time.

Key Notes 3.1

1. Repeated stimulation of the siphon of *Aplysia* leads to a decrease in the amplitude of the gill-retraction reflex that is evoked by this stimulus.
2. A period free from stimulation is said to cause spontaneous recovery, in that a subsequent stimulus evokes an enhanced response.
3. Following habituation, a strong tactile stimulus (B) to the head causes sensitization. This is revealed as follows. The magnitude of the gill-retraction response to the original stimulus (A), to which the system has habituated, is increased immediately following B. This behavioural phenomenon is termed dishabituation.
4. Closure of calcium channels in the presynaptic membrane of the sensory neuron forms the cellular basis of habituation. Their reopening (sensitization) is the basis of dishabituation.
5. A serotoninergic interneuron is responsibile for opening of calcium channels.

3.2   The Visual System

Diagnostic Questions for Section 3.2

1. What is a light receptor?
2. In the visual system, what is a receptive field?
3. A change in activity of a ganglion cell with respect to its spontaneous firing rate might be carrying what information?

Between the arrival of light at the eye and its perception, there lie complex circuits of neurons. We are in a position to understand how some of the stages of processing work. To do so, a knowledge of the characteristics of individual neurons is vital.

Light that is either emitted by objects or reflected from them impinges upon the *retina,* which forms the inner lining of the eye (Fig. 3.7). Here an image of the object is formed upon the mosaic of light *receptors* that cover the retina (Fig. 3.8). These receptors are basically of two kinds: *rods* and *cones.* Receptors are a type of small nerve cell, not having the extensive processes described for the classical neuron in the last module (Fig. 3.9). On absorbing incoming light, receptors change their electrical state (membrane potential). This ability of receptors to absorb light and thereby change their electrical state is a necessary condition for the perception of visual form; it is the first stage of visual processing.

These receptors are linked by synapses to *bipolar cells* (Fig. 3.9). A change in electrical state at the receptor will, in turn, change the electrical state of the associated bipolar cell. At the third stage in the sequence the bipolar cells then synapse upon, and influence, *ganglion cells.* It is only at this third stage, in the ganglion cells, that action

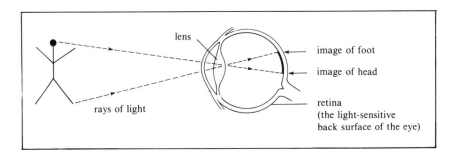

Figure 3.7   The relationship between an object in the world and the image on the retina. Light rays coming from the object are brought to a focus on the retina; that is, an image is formed. This image is upside down. (Source: SD286, Module B2.)

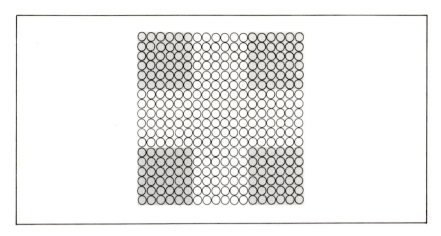

Figure 3.8   An area of retina, part of which is in darkness and part of which is illuminated by a white cross. Note the population of receptors that form a mosaic covering the retina. The receptor population corresponding to the cross will signal the presence of light in that region.
(Source: SD286, Module B2.)

potentials appear. For the transfers: receptor→bipolar cell and bipolar cell→ganglion cell, even in the absence of action potentials, a change in the electrical state of one cell causes a change in the state of the cell with which it synapses. (However, elsewhere in the nervous system, for transfer of information over anything but very short distances, action potentials are employed.) Usually a large population of receptors converge, via their associated bipolar cell, upon a single ganglion cell.

The axons of the many ganglion cells (whose cell bodies are at the retina) together constitute the optic nerve (Fig. 3.10). Action potentials, generated in the ganglion cells, travel along the axons that form the optic nerve (G), and synapse with neurons in the lateral geniculate nucleus (D). These lateral geniculate nucleus neurons project their axons (B) to the visual cortex of the brain (C). Action potentials are thus conveyed to the visual cortex.

Research on the visual system has been characterized by considerable success in explaining some important features and components of the processing system. In particular, we understand rather well some of the early stages in the sequence of processing. Some aspects of visual perception, known from psychological investigation, can be given a neurophysiological embodiment in terms of the interactions between nerve cells. The notion of *receptive field* is central to such investigation.

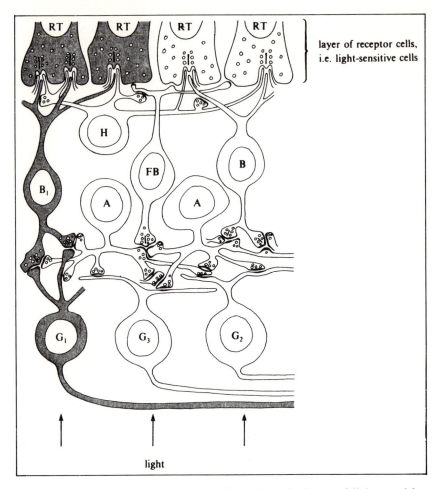

layer of receptor cells, i.e. light-sensitive cells

light

Figure 3.9 A section through the retina. Note the layer of light-sensitive cells, the receptors (RT) and the layer of ganglion cells (G1, G2, etc.). Two receptors, shaded grey, are shown to be influencing the activity of a bipolar cell (B1). This cell in turn activates a particular ganglion cell G1. Note that although the absorption of light by the receptors is the first stage of visual processing, light in fact has to pass through the ganglion and bipolar layers before reaching the receptors. In other words; you might say that the retina is inside-out.
(Source: SD286, Module B2.)

The term 'receptive field' is used to describe an area of sensory surface that is able to influence the activity of a particular neuron that we have chosen to study. In the case of the tactile sense, this

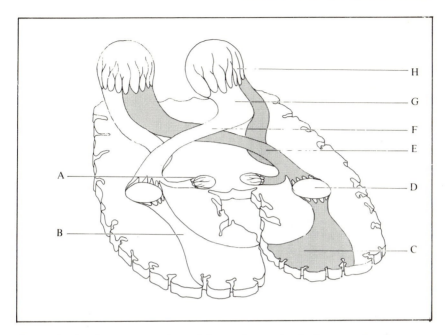

Figure 3.10   A representation of the pathways in the human visual system.
A = superior colliculus; B = optic radiations; C = area 17 (visual or striate
cortex); D = lateral geniculate nucleus; E = optic tract; F = optic chiasma;
G = optic nerve fibres; H = retina. The grey-coloured pathway represents
that which conveys information to the *right* hemisphere of the brain (to the
visual cortex of this hemisphere). Note that such information arises from
receptors in the *right* half of the retina of each of the two eyes. The white
pathway represents information directed to the left half of the visual cortex.
Note that such information arises from the left half of the retina of each
eye. Note the cross-over of some pathways at the optic chiasma.
(Source: SD286, Module C7.)

would refer to an area of skin, contact with which can influence the
activity of a particular sensory neuron. For vision, consider one of
the many ganglion cells whose axons form the optic nerve. Among
the light receptors at the retina, a certain population, acting via their
associated bipolar cells, will be able to influence the firing activity of
the particular ganglion cell under consideration. That is to say, light
falling upon the area of retina defined by this population of receptors
will be able to change the ganglion cell's firing level.

Ganglion cells show a certain *spontaneous* rate of discharge of
action potentials even in total darkness. Therefore, to say that light
falling within the receptive field might influence the ganglion cell,

is to allow for the possibility that the influence could be one of increasing or decreasing firing level relative to the spontaneous rate.

In the absence of a detailed anatomical wiring diagram showing the interconnections between the relevant neurons, how might we determine the receptive field of a particular ganglion cell? Hubel and Wiesel (1959) devised a technique for this, as shown in Techniques Box C.

Techniques Box C

Defining the receptive field

A cat is anaesthetized and placed before a screen, with its head held in a fixed position (Fig. 3.11). Hence, a fixed relationship between the surface of the screen and the retinal surface can be assumed; that is, a given location on the screen always corresponds to a given location on the retinal surface.

According to its exact position, a recording electrode can be made to pick up the activity of a *single* ganglion cell. It is found that even in total darkness a ganglion cell will typically show a certain level of *spontaneous activity*; that is to say, the rate of generation of action potentials in the ganglion will not be zero. A small 'pencil' of light is then projected onto the screen and moved around until a change in the electrical activity of the ganglion cell is observed. The area of screen within which light is able to influence the cell in question defines its receptive field. Typically, it is found that, within a certain area of screen, when light is turned *on*, the cell will increase its firing rate (relative to the spontaneous level). This area of the screen, and hence the corresponding area of the retina, is defined as the ON region of the ganglion cell. For stimulation at certain other regions of the screen, the ganglion cell will *decrease* its rate of firing when the light is turned on. However, in such a region, it will increase its rate of firing to above the spontaneous activity level when the light is turned OFF. Hence, such a region is termed an OFF region. The receptive field is made up of the ON and OFF regions. Regions of the screen where the light causes no change in firing rate of the ganglion cell relative to its spontaneous level are defined as being outside of its receptive field.

Ganglion cells often have a receptive field of the form of an ON circle surrounded by an OFF annulus. Figure 3.12 shows the responses of such a ganglion cell to light onset and off-set in the two regions of its receptive field. The opposite type of cell is also found: an OFF centre and ON surround.

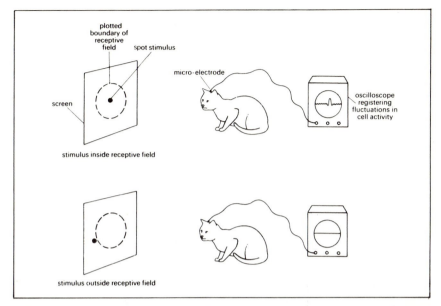

Figure 3.11   Technique for recording the electrical activity of an individual cell in the visual system. A small pencil of light (spot stimulus) is moved around on the screen. Electrical activity of the cell is noted for various positions of the spot on the screen. The area of screen that can influence the cell defines its receptive field. The receptive field is normally composed of ON and OFF areas. Areas outside the receptive field, by definition, are ineffective in influencing the cell.

(Source: Greene and Hicks, 1984.)

SAQ 30
In order to maximize the electrical activity of an ON centre/OFF-surround ganglion cell, what would you judge to be the optimal light stimulus?

A high rate of generation of action potentials in the ganglion cell of Figure 3.12 carries important information: that a spot of light with a dark surround is present at a *particular location* on the retina.

SAQ 31
Light impinging upon the retina can cause a decrease in the firing rate of a ganglion cell to below its spontaneous level. What does this suggest regarding the processes of interaction between cells described in Module 2?

57

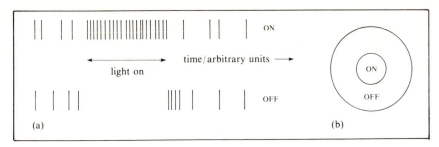

Figure 3.12   Responses of a ganglion cell. (a) The top trace shows the frequency of action potentials arising in a ganglion cell when a spot of light falling in the ON region is turned on and then turned off. Note the initial background level of firing of the ganglion cell. Turning the light on increases the frequency of generation of action potentials to above this spontaneous level. Turning the light off temporarily reduces activity to below its background level. The lower trace shows what happens when the spot of light is projected onto the off region of the cell. Note the *suppression* of activity to below its background level for the period that the light is on. Note also the increase in activity of the ganglion cell when the light is turned off. (b) The receptive field of the ganglion cell whose activity is shown in (a). A centre ON region is surrounded by an annular OFF region. (Source: SD286, Module B1.)

Look back to Figure 3.9 (p. 54). So far I have described how stimulation of receptors in the ON area of the receptive field of a ganglion cell, stimulate bipolars, which, in turn, excite the ganglion. In order to explain how stimulation of receptor cells lying in the OFF part of the receptive field can inhibit the same ganglion cell, we need to consider a different route. The receptors in the OFF region activate a *horizontal cell* (H), and activity in this cell exerts an inhibitory effect in the pathway.

Figure 3.13 shows the relevance of these models to visual perception. Suppose that the area defined by the population of receptors shown (e.g. R_1, R_2) constitutes the receptive field of a ganglion cell. The inner circle (bounded by the dotted line) might be an OFF area and the area that surrounds this circle, the annulus, an ON area. Onset of a light stimulus taking the form of the annulus shown would excite the cell. The area of medium intensity light, shown as the uniform grey stimulus, would have little or no effect, even though, on average, it might contain as much light energy as the annulus.

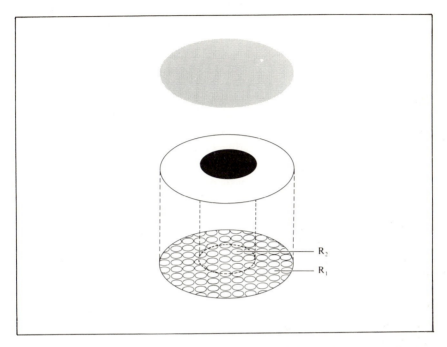

Figure 3.13   An area of retina showing a population of receptor cells that make up the receptive field of a particular OFF-centre/ON-surround ganglion cell. Receptor cells such as R1 are part of the ON region. Light falling on them tends to excite the ganglion cell. Receptor cells such as R2 are part of the OFF region; light falling on such cells activates an inhibitory influence on the particular ganglion cell. Consider two possible visual stimuli that can be applied to this receptive field. First, the light annulus with dark centre shown just above the retina would excite such a ganglion cell. However, a uniform stimulus extending over the grey area (shown at the top) would be relatively ineffective in changing its activity level.
(Source: SD286, Module B2).

SAQ 32
Why would the medium intensity stimulus have relatively little effect on the ganglion cell in question?

For a particular ganglion cell, R_1 might, as described, exert an excitatory effect and R_2 an inhibitory effect. However, receptors usually make numerous connections. Another ganglion cell might be excited by R_2 and inhibited by R_1. In other words, the retinal surface that forms the receptive field of a given ganglion cell does not exclusively provide the receptive field of that cell and none other. Rather, multiple representations of the receptor surface are involved.

Extensive investigation of ganglion cells has found their receptive fields to be circular, with either an ON centre and OFF surround or OFF centre and ON surround. Suppose now we move deeper into the visual system, and, with an electrode, probe the *visual cortex*, a region of brain concerned with vision (see Figure 3.10). Here we find receptive fields of a different form to those found earlier in the visual pathways. Instead of the circular ON/OFF receptive field that is characteristic of ganglion cells and those in the lateral geniculate nucleus, more complex patterns of light are usually needed in order to trigger cortical cells. For example, a *slit* of light falling at a particular location and orientation on the retina might constitute the cortical cell's receptive field. In other words, the optimal stimulus to maximize the activity in such a cell would be a slit of light just filling this area. A spot of light would be relatively ineffective in stimulating such a cell.

By examining the receptive field characteristics of cells in the visual system, we can see some of the basic features of visual perception appearing. For instance, we know that the visual system is particularly sensitive to contours, regions of contrasting illumination, such as spots, corners, edges, and so on. Even at an early stage in processing visual information—the ganglion-cell level—there is clear evidence of responsiveness to contrast and insensitivity to diffuse illumination.

The perception of objects that we see around us involves processes at various levels in the nervous system. Memory of past events, expectations concerning the world and reconstruction of fragmentary information all play essential roles in determining how we perceive. At present most of these processes lie beyond the reach of an analysis made at the level of nerve-cell interactions.

The term 'top-down' was used in Module 1 to describe a level of explanation. A different, but analogous, way in which the expression is employed is in the context of perception. One can consider the brain to impose 'top-down' an interpretation upon information coming from the eyes. Such information is vital to the perceptual process, but it has to be put into context. Perception is the outcome of a complex system of which information derived from the image at the retina is only a part. For example, look at Figure 3.14. What do you see? I'd guess that sometimes you will see it as a rabbit and at other times as a duck. There is only one image on the retina, and hence only one source of information to the brain, but two possible interpretations are applied to this data. This is described as the brain imposing interpretations 'top-down' onto the raw sensory data.

Figure 3.14   Rabbit/duck illusion. Sometimes the figure is seen as a duck and sometimes as a rabbit.
(Source: SD286, Module C7.)

Key Notes 3.2

1. Light is absorbed by receptors and thereby changes their membrane potential. This is the first stage of the process of visual perception.
2. Receptors synapse upon bipolar cells.
3. Bipolar cells synapse upon ganglion cells.
4. The receptive field of a ganglion cell is that area of retina upon which the impingement of light can change the activity level of the ganglion cell. Within the ON region, light will increase the ganglion cell's firing level. Within the OFF region, the onset of light will decrease it to below its spontaneous level.
5. The optimal stimulus to activate a ganglion cell is light filling its ON region and not invading its OFF region.
6. By looking at the response characteristics of identifiable cells within the visual system, one can begin to see some of the bases of perceptual phenomena.

3.3   Responses to Tissue Damage

Diagnostic Questions for Section 3.3

1. What is a nociceptor?
2. In what way does the nociceptor differ from the textbook neuron?
3. Distinguish between the mode of action of aspirin and lignocaine.

The mechanism of pain serves to protect the body. We tend to remove the body from a damaging stimulus, such as a hot object or a thorn. Some pains cause us to rest, and hence they aid recuperation. We can understand some important features of the pain mechanisms by looking at some of the neurons involved.

When body tissue is damaged (e.g. by cutting or burning) receptors that are specialized to detect such damage are stimulated. These receptors are known as *nociceptors* (meaning, concerned with tissue damage and pain). Figure 3.15 shows in schematic form what is happening. Note that the nociceptor does not conform to the standard neuron described in Module 2. It has one long axon-like process that runs from the periphery (in this case, the skin) to the spinal cord. The cell body, rather than being at one end of the cell, is to one side. (In this respect, the nociceptor's form is typical of sensory neurons that bring information from the skin to the spinal cord). This is one example of the differences in neuronal form that exist in the nervous system (see Sect. 2.3).

Tissue damage in the vicinity of the tip of the nociceptor causes the generation of action potentials that travel to the spinal cord. At the spinal cord, the nociceptor makes a synapse with another cell. This cell might then project its axon directly up to the brain, carrying the

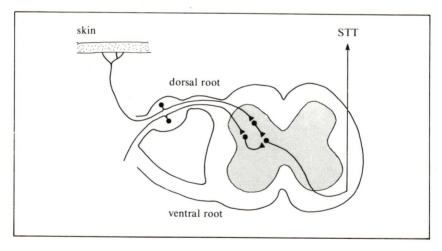

Figure 3.15 Tissue-damage detection. A nociceptor whose cell body is in the dorsal root ganglion (indicated by a black blob) conveys information from the skin to the spinal cord (shown in cross-section). Note the ending of the nociceptor at the skin. It is this ending that is sensitive to tissue damage. The noxious information after reaching the spinal cord is then carried towards the brain. In this case it is shown to be carried in the white matter of the spinal cord by an axon forming part of the *spinothalamic tract* (STT).

(Source: SD286, Module C6.)

information that tissue damage is occurring at a particular location in the body. Alternatively, as shown in Figure 3.15, the nociceptor might first synapse upon one cell, this second cell then synapses upon a third, and the axon of the third cell projects up to the brain.

A nociceptor has a relatively high *threshold*, meaning that it is usually relatively difficult to cause it to fire. Such stimuli as, say, a light touch in its receptive field are ineffective. This would of course have to be the case for the cell to serve its role as a detector of tissue damage.

It is sometimes tempting to refer to the nociceptor as a 'pain detector'. This expression might sometimes provide a useful short-hand but can lead to serious confusion and is best avoided. First, pain is not a stimulus, but rather a perceptual experience generated in some circumstances by particular stimuli. The mechanism responsible for pain represents a complex system, involving such behaviours as withdrawal from the aversive stimulus and intense emotional expression. To the conscious human, pain has of course a vivid personal affective value. These consequences of tissue damage depend upon the processing of information at various levels in the nervous system, the first stage of which is normally provided by the nociceptors. To call the nociceptor a pain detector might suggest a simple one-to-one relationship between its activity and the pain reaction. No such simple relationship exists. Sometimes pain is experienced in the apparent absence of nociceptor input; for example, in the phenomenon of *phantom-limb pain*. In this situation, pain is felt and perceived as coming from a limb that no longer exists (e.g. following surgical amputation). Conversely, even in the conscious human, tissue damage does not invariably lead to a corresponding amount of pain. Injuries incurred during sports or in battle have sometimes been reported to be free of pain. Nonetheless, under most circumstances actual or incipient tissue damage is a necessary and sufficient condition for pain and the associated reactions.

SAQ 33

Can you suggest an analogy between (1) the relationship between tissue damage, the nociceptor and pain and (2) light, receptors in the eye and visual perception? Consider carefully the appropriate terminology in each case.

A significant effort on the part of medical science is of course devoted to the alleviation of pain. We are able to understand some of the mechanisms of pain relief in terms of the nociceptor.

SAQ 34
Consider the nociceptor detecting tissue damage, transmitting this information and then, via the synapse that it makes, conveying it to another cell for transmission to the brain (see Fig. 3.15). In principle, where, in this pathway, could *analgesic* (pain relieving) substances work?

For example, *aspirin* exerts its analgesic effect by making it less likely that action potentials will arise in the nociceptor. The local anaesthetic *lignocaine*, which you might have received at the dentist, works by impeding the passage of action potentials along the nociceptor axon. It does this by blocking sodium channels in the nerve cell membrane. Since sodium is unable to enter the cell, it means that the action potential cannot pass the point affected by lignocaine.

SAQ 35
In visiting the dentist, have you noticed one of the side effects of the use of lignocaine as an analgesic? How might this be explained?

It is also possible to reduce pain by blocking transmission at the synapses in the spinal cord that form part of the nociceptive (i.e. concerned with tissue damage and pain) pathway. Drugs known as *opiates* (e.g. morphine) act at this level in the system (as well as at other sites). Specific receptors for opiates have been found in the central nervous system, and this is an area of intense research.

If all else fails, surgery is sometimes used in an attempt to counter chronic pain. This consists in cutting fibre tracts implicated in carrying noxious information (e.g. spino-thalamic tract; see Fig. 3.15). The effects of such surgery are very mixed; often the pain reappears. Even brain surgery is sometimes employed. Following such surgery, patients sometimes report that the pain is still present in terms of its sensory qualities, but its emotional value has been diminished.

Key Notes 3.3

1. A nociceptor is sensitive to tissue damage occurring in its receptive field.
2. Tissue damage instigates action potentials in the nociceptor. These travel to the spinal cord, where the nociceptor forms a

synapse with another cell that carries 'noxious information' to the brain.

3. Pain relief can sometimes be obtained by means of diminishing the input from the nociceptor to its associated cell.

Reading Guide

Kandel, E. R. and Schwartz, J. H. (1982). Molecular biology of learning: Modulation of transmitter release, *Science*, 218, 433–43.

Kuffler, S. W. and Nicholls, J. G. (1977) *From Neuron to Brain*, Sunderland, Sinauer.

Melzack, R. and Wall, P. (1984) *The Challenge of Pain*, Harmondsworth, Penguin.

Open University *SD286, Biology, Brain and Behaviour,* Modules B2, C6, C7, Milton Keynes, Open University Educational Enterprises.

4 Learning and Memory Module

Link from Neuronal Systems Module to Learning and Memory

In the last module, we described habituation in *Aplysia*. The animal's response to a given stimulus changes over time, as a function of its previous experience. This represents a simple case of learning. The cellular bases of habituation (e.g. a change in the opening of calcium channels), in a sense, represent a memory of past stimuli that have resulted in habituation. This module looks in more detail at learning and memory.

The last module showed where a knowledge of the properties of the nerve cell and of how nerve cells form systems can be used to illuminate phenomena at the behavioural level. However, apart from the study of *Aplysia*, we concentrated upon the input side to the nervous system (i.e. the first stages in the processing of visual and noxious information). It is at this level that we have gained most insight from looking at complex neural systems.

This module looks at what are essentially central processes: learning and memory. We shall be concerned with animals having more complex nervous systems than *Aplysia*; for example, rats, birds and humans. Our ability to use an understanding of neurons and how they form systems is perhaps less impressive here than in the domains discussed in the last Module. However, consideration of possible neuronal networks is still central to the discussion. This module will emphasize the theme introduced in Module 1 that different levels of explanation can be brought to the study of a given phenomenon.

General Diagnostic Questions for Learning and Memory

1. Why is the study of learning and memory very much a multidisciplinary one? (Sect. 4.1).
2. What are some of the similarities and differences in the procedure and outcome of classical and operant conditioning? (Sect. 4.2).
3. Do we now need to abandon the search for general principles of learning? (Sect. 4.3.)
4. Why might it be said that memory is sometimes fragile? (Sect. 4.4.)
5. What is the relevance of the synapse to the study of memory? (Sect. 4.5)

4.1 Definitions and Levels of Analysis

Diagnostic Questions for Section 4.1

1. What is learning?
2. What is memory?
3. Why should a biochemist be interested in memory?

Learning and memory present a very good example of how a phenomenon in the area of brain and behaviour can be studied at more than one level. Biochemists, neurophysiologists, psychologists and ethologists each have a characteristic point of view and research strategy concerning what is important to them. These views are usually not to be taken as rival accounts for the truth. Rather, each discipline tends to look at a different level or aspect of roughly the same phenomenon.

More than some of the other topics that we consider here (e.g. vision or the motivational bases of drinking), the phenomena of learning and memory pose particularly awkward questions of definition. What exactly is learning? What constitutes a memory? Of course, we all have a 'commonsense' answer to these questions, but finding a scientifically rigorous definition is difficult. Not all definitions that the reader is likely to encounter will necessarily agree. For example, different schools within psychology—such as cognitive psychology (emphasizing cognitions) and radical behaviourism (emphasizing actual behaviour—would be expected to show considerable divergence of opinion).

Perhaps we could try, somewhat provisionally, the following definitions. 'Learning' is the process of acquiring information regarding the presence of, and relationship between, events in the world. By 'events', one must include relationships between muscular actions and their outcome, such as playing tennis. 'Memory' is the process involved in *storing* such information. Learning can concern purely external events (e.g. a left turn in the maze leads to food; thunder follows lightning) or also involve internal events (e.g. the taste of certain food is followed by illness). Whatever the level of analysis, the essence of learning is *change*. The change might take the form of a different responsiveness to the external world, a different expectation about the immediate future or different behaviour. Such changes are assumed to be based upon changes in the nervous system resulting from *experience*.

Learning is sometimes described as an example of the *plasticity* of the nervous system. The ability to change behaviour in the light of experience confers some rather obvious advantages upon an animal. For example, suppose a rat encounters a novel food; following ingestion it might become ill, or it might derive beneficial nutritional consequences. Either way, its future reaction to the same food needs to take cognizance of past experience: to reject or to ingest the particular food. Learning confers *flexibility*: the animal can adjust its reactions according to circumstances. The alternative is to have an inflexible nervous system, unable to adapt to changing circumstances. An animal equipped with such a nervous system would come into the world with a predetermined set of solutions. For example, it would accept or reject a particular food on the basis of taste; there would be no possibility of the strategy 'suck it and see'. Such a strategy might well suffice for certain species in particular stable environments. However, an opportunistic animal such as the rat needs to have a learning capacity.

Although, for the convenience of study, we often need to draw a distinction between learning and memory, we must be careful not to overstate the distinction. For some purposes it might prove more useful to view learning and memory as two *aspects* of the one system of information assimilation. However, for other purposes we do need to divide the system up into processes or stages, even though the way that we make our divisions might later appear to be somewhat arbitrary. As a first approximation, it can be useful to think of three stages involved in memory: (1) formation, (2) retention and (3) retrieval (Squire and Cohen, 1984). Such a division has proven useful for understanding the nature of some memory deficits shown by patients (e.g. disease syndromes). Suppose someone is suffering from a memory fault. Let us consider the three possible types of deficiency to which our classification leads us. First, information might not have been assimilated into a memory as well as for normal control subjects. Second, the memory might have been formed normally in the first place, but retained poorly. Metaphorically speaking, it might have 'leaked away'. The third possibility is that memory is stored normally, but the subject is unable to recall the memory. Some process might be blocking retrieval. We need to be careful not to consider these as necessarily mutually exclusive possibilities, but the categorization is often useful. We also have to be aware that different forms of memory might be differently affected by any given disease condition (Squire and Cohen, 1984).

For obvious reasons, learning and memory form an object of study for the psychologist. However, we assume that memory is embodied in some kind of change in the physical structure of the brain, involving nerve cell interactions, hence the relevance of biochemistry and neurophysiology.

Key Notes 4.1

1. Learning refers to the acquisition of information, and memory refers to its storage.
2. Different disciplines look at different aspects of learning and memory.
3. The physical embodiment of memory, in the form of a structural change in the brain, is the object of study by biochemists.

4.2 Approaches to Learning

Diagnostic Questions for Section 4.2

1. In what sense might the effect of a tone used in a classical conditioning experiment be described as 'conditional'?
2. Distinguish between the two related meanings of 'extinction'— as a procedure and as a behavioural outcome.
3. Distinguish between positive reinforcement, negative reinforcement and punishment.
4. How might one ascertain objectively whether a given event constitutes positive reinforcement or punishment?

The two major classes of learning studied by psychologists are classical and instrumental conditioning. This section looks at each of these in turn.

Take an external event that has been demonstrated to have relatively little significance for a food-deprived dog; for example, a tone or a light. Let us say that we have found that a tone provokes the dog to make merely a slight investigation of its source, the loudspeaker. Then, on several occasions, follow the presentation of the tone, one second later, with food. In the famous experiment by Pavlov, it was found that, after a few such pairings, the tone *on its own* was able to elicit salivation. In the language of contemporary learning theory, it would be said that the dog had learned an *expectation* of food, aroused by the tone (Dickinson, 1980; Toates, 1986). In more conventional language, as developed by Pavlov, we would describe the various factors as follows (Fig. 4.1). Food is the unconditional stimulus (UCS). That is to say, food unconditionally elicits salivation; its power to do so does not depend upon prior pairing with another stimulus (some writers use the term 'unconditioned' rather than 'unconditional'). The salivation caused by food presenta-

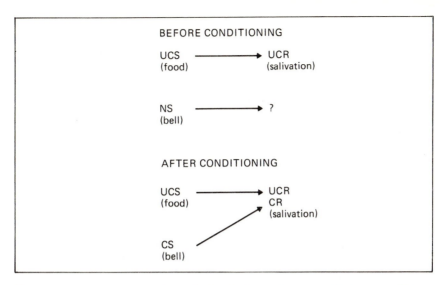

Figure 4.1   A representation of classical conditioning. Before conditioning, a neutral stimulus (NS), in this case a bell, does not evoke salivation. It might evoke some kind of orientation reaction. An unconditional stimulus (UCS), food, evokes an unconditional response (UCR), salivation. After conditioning, the UCS evokes the same UCR, but now the NS (termed CS) is able to evoke a conditional response (CR). This consists of salivation and is similar to the salivation caused by the UCS.
(Source: Greene and Hicks, 1984.)

tion is termed the *unconditional response* (UCR). Following pairing with food, the tone is known as the *conditional stimulus* (CS). This expression conveys the meaning that the stimulus is able to evoke the response in question only by virtue of its earlier pairing with the UCS. The tone owes its power to elicit salivation to ('is conditional upon') its association with food; it is not an intrinsic property of the tone. The term *conditional response* (CR) refers to the response evoked by the conditional stimulus; in the present case this is a flow of saliva. The response to this particular stimulus is conditional upon the prior tone–food pairing.

Although the conditional response often looks very much like the unconditional response, it is important to make the distinction. For example, in a salivary conditioning experiment, slightly less saliva would typically be evoked by the tone than by the food. In other situations, following conditioning, the CR is very different from the UCR.

SAQ 36
A certain child is observed to show fear reactions to the sight of a snake. These consist of heart rate acceleration, sweating and trembling. The same child enjoys visiting his uncle Tom's house. One day, uncle Tom buys a pet snake, and puts it in a cage in the living room. On subsequent occasions, on arriving at the front door of the house the child experiences fear. Describe this situation in terms of classical conditioning, and define the UCS, UCR, CS and CR.

Instrumental conditioning is the second of the major techniques of conditioning. We can best illustrate this by contrasting it with classical conditioning. In the classical conditioning of, say, salivation, the two events that became paired, the tone and the food, were presented at a time selected by the experimenter; that is, the dog was not an active agent in the causation of either the bell or the food. On a given conditioning trial, it did not have to behave in any particular way for either to appear. By contrast, for instrumental conditioning, the animal's own behaviour on a particular occasion plays a role in what happens, and thereby in the learning process. Behaviour is *instrumental* in obtaining a particular outcome. For example, in a typical experiment in the *Skinner-box*, a rat gets a pellet of food each time it presses a lever. It might be said to acquire an association between its behaviour and the consequence. Similarly, it might learn that turning left in a T-maze leads to ('is instrumental in getting to') food.

In both the classical and instrumental conditioning experiments that we have described, food is often termed a *reinforcer*. This expression refers to the agent that strengthens an association. For example, if a hungry rat obtains food by turning left in a maze, this outcome strengthens ('reinforces') the future tendency to turn left when the rat is placed in the same situation. In the case of classical conditioning, repeated pairing of bell and food strengthens the bell's power to induce salivation. Therefore, although we are dealing with two quite different techniques, several similar principles apply and, to some extent, a common terminology is used.

For both classical and instrumental conditioning, if, following learning, the animal is placed in the experimental test situation but reinforcement is not given, this constitutes the application of *extinction* conditions. Since we have considered the case of food as reinforcer for both classical and instrumental conditioning, it will be convenient to remain with these examples. For classical conditioning, the amount of saliva provoked by the bell will decline. Similarly, for an instrumentally acquired habit, the animal will, for example, slow up and finally cease running in a maze. The respective habits would then be said to be *extinguished*. Note that the habit is only extinguished after a period during which extinction *conditions* have been applied. Despite several parallels between classical and instrumental conditioning, and the use of some common expressions, it is important to keep the difference in the training procedures in mind.

SAQ 37

A rat has been trained in a Skinner-box to obtain the reward of a pellet of food for bar-pressing. How would you apply extinction conditions, and what criterion would you adopt in order to define when the habit is extinguished?

Although it was convenient throughout to use mainly food as an example of a reinforcer, there is a variety of other possible reinforcers available. For example, as we saw in SAQ 36, in classical conditioning, an innocuous object paired with a fear-evoking object can acquire fear-evoking properties. In instrumental conditioning, food, water, sex or the attention of someone are all possible reinforcers.

SAQ 38

Go back and have another look at SAQ 36. How would you impose extinction conditions in this situation, and what would be your index of when the conditioning is *in fact* extinguished?

In instrumental conditioning, the subject's behaviour can lead to either the *gain* or the *loss* of something. The term *positive reinforcement* refers to the gain of, say, food or water, *contingent* upon execution of a particular response. Such positive reinforcers as food or water increase the frequency of the behaviour upon which their presentation is contingent. For example, suppose a child is given praise each time he or she is helpful in the kitchen. For praise to constitute a positive reinforcer, the frequency of doing such work would have to *increase* above its initial base-line level.

A *negative reinforcer* is something whose *termination* increases the frequency of behaviour on which the termination is contingent. For example, terminating an unpleasantly loud sound might be made contingent upon a bar-press in a Skinner-box. Sometimes aversive events such as electric shocks are termed *negative reinforcers*, referring to their properties. Unfortunately, confusion can easily enter at this point, since such events can serve two quite distinct roles. First, they can indeed be used in a negative reinforcement contingency, as just described. However, they can also be used in a contingency of *punishment*, where they are caused to *appear*, rather than terminate, following a particular response. For example, if an animal has established the habit of bar-pressing for food, and then an electric shock rather than food is given for making the bar-press, this changes a contingency of positive reinforcement into one of punishment. The rat would *decrease* its rate of bar-pressing. By contrast, if the experiment were set up such that, by bar-pressing, the rat could terminate a shock, this would constitute negative reinforcement. One might expect the frequency of bar-pressing to increase under such a contingency.

SAQ 39

How might one objectively measure whether stroking an animal is an example of punishment or positive reinforcement?

SAQ 40

In an instrumental conditioning experiment, would a loud noise constitute a punishment or a negative reinforcement?

The distinction between punishment and negative reinforcement can be made in terms of the contingency in use. However, very often the distinction between positive and negative reinforcement is somewhat arbitrary. For example, is the injection of heroin by an addict an example of positive reinforcement (i.e. the temporary attainment of euphoria) or negative reinforcement (i.e. escape from the painful withdrawal symptoms of heroin)? In such cases, it is perhaps most accurate to see reinforcement as an inevitable interaction between positive and negative aspects.

SAQ 41

A child is bored to tears learning French grammar. Each time the child throws a missile across the room, it is sent out of the class. Interpret these events in terms of positive reinforcement, negative reinforcement and punishment.

Western and Soviet research on learning have tended to diverge since Pavlov. Soviet investigators have shown a particular interest in the brain mechanisms underlying classical conditioning. They have investigated possible changes in connections between nerve cells that underlie formation of the learned association (see later in this Module). In Eastern Europe, studies of conditioning are carried out in neural science departments. In the West, learning has been studied primarily in psychology laboratories, often with no reference to the underlying biological mechanisms. In the West, there has been more emphasis upon instrumental conditioning than in the USSR.

Key Notes 4.2

1. Classical conditioning consists in pairing a neutral stimulus (NS) with a stimulus of some significance (UCS) that elicits an UCR. By virtue of the pairing, the CS is able to elicit a CR that is similar in some respects to the UCR.
2. Instrumental conditioning depends upon an animal, by its own action, causing something significant to happen. An association is formed between the action and the consequence.
3. Extinction conditions are where a reinforcer is omitted. The acquired habit will then usually extinguish.
4. A positive reinforcer is something that increases the frequency of the behaviour upon which its presentation is contingent (e.g. food). A negative reinforcer is something that increases the frequency of behaviour when termination of the reinforcer is contingent upon behaviour (e.g. termination of a loud noise). Punishment is something that decreases the frequency of behaviour upon which its presentation is contingent (e.g. presentation of shock).

4.3 A Natural History Approach

Diagnostic Questions for Section 4.3

1. What is the Garcia effect, and what is its significance?
2. In what ways can the evolution and life-style of a species be related to its learning capacity?

In the history of experimental psychology, there has been considerable enthusiasm for the idea that *general laws of learning* can be applied. Such general models have been couched in terms of classical and instrumental conditioning. This search for parsimony was particularly evident in the period from 1920 to 1970. This approach has been characterized by the notion that there exist general laws applicable to any situation and species. Hence little concern with species differences has been shown. In parallel, there has often been a lack of attention towards the particular combination of reponse and reinforcer employed in a given learning task. For example, theorists might have assumed implicitly that, if the frequency of bar-pressing in rats can be increased by making food contingent upon this response, one could also increase, say, the frequency of face-washing in hamsters by use of the same reinforcer. However, over the years, an increasing number of awkward 'exceptions' to such general principles have appeared, together with some 'dissident' psychologists, urging that we pay attention to species differences. These days, an increasing number of investigators, guided by zoological considerations of species differences, pay particular attention to *differences* in learning mechanisms and capacities.

In the classical experiment by Pavlov, the food was presented at about one second after the bell was sounded. If the interval between CS and UCS was made somewhat longer than this, conditioning became impossible. This effect, obtained also in other classical conditioning experiments, led to the general conclusion that conditioning requires a close association in time between CS and UCS. The generality of this assumption seemed to extend to instrumental conditioning. For example, if food does not appear almost immediately upon arriving in a goal-box, it is very difficult to train an animal to follow a route to the goal-box.

In the 1960s, an experiment was reported that was to shatter our cosy set of assumptions regarding generality. Using rats, John Garcia (see e.g. Garcia, Clarke and Hankins, 1973) tried pairing a particular taste with ill-effects (nausea) experienced an hour or more after sampling the taste. He found that rats very readily developed an aversion to the taste. Subsequently, they refused to ingest a substance having this taste. Furthermore, such long-delay conditioning was peculiar to an association with *taste* If a particular visual stimulus were presented at the time of ingestion, there was relatively little aversive association formed with this stimulus.

SAQ 42

By what objective criteria might one compare the strength of association formed with a taste and with a visual stimulus?

The phenomenon of a selective association between a particular stimulus and ill-effects, bridging a long interval between the two events, has become known as the *Garcia effect*.

Subsequent research has revealed some important species differences. Some species of bird readily form an association between a *visual* stimulus and ill-effects experienced much later. Thus, in defining the parameters of possible association formation, we need to look at both the timing and the nature of the two events that we pair. The evolution and life-style of a species might be expected to relate to its learning capacities. In selecting food in their natural environment, rats probably rely upon smell and taste more than visual cues. Birds, having a more developed visual sense and often ingesting brightly coloured fruits and insects, exploit vision in food selection.

Can we fit taste-aversion learning into either of the two paradigms of learning described earlier? On balance the phenomenon is generally considered to be a specialized form of classical conditioning; that is, a previously innocuous taste takes on an aversive quality by virtue of its pairing with nausea. The rat does not even need to ingest the substance to develop an aversion. It can be formed even if the odour is simply wafted across the animal's nose, and followed by illness.

SAQ 43
Suppose we apply the classical conditioning model to taste-aversion learning. What is the UCS, CS, UCR, and CR? In what way might the distinction between UCR and CR (described earlier, p. 71) be relevant?

The expression *constraints on learning* is now commonly used as a counterbalance to the blanket assumptions that (1) all animals are alike in their learning capacities, and (2) any arbitrary event can equally well be associated with any event significant to the animal. However, a compromise position is perhaps the safest to hold. It is still useful to look for some simple and general principles of learning, but these are bound to need careful qualification and adaptation to each particular situation. For example, salivary conditioning and taste-aversion learning both have important common features (e.g. acquisition of a capacity as a result of an association with a significant event), despite a vast difference in time parameters.

Key Notes 4.3

1. Although some general principles of learning are still valid, we need to qualify them according to the species and situation.
2. In rats, an association between taste and illness can readily be

formed, despite the passage of hours between taste and ill-effects.

3. Other species more readily associate visual cues with long-delayed nausea.

4.4 Psychological and Neurophysiological Approaches to Memory

Diagnostic Questions for Section 4.4

1. What do we mean by the term 'decay' of memory?
2. What is retrograde amnesia, and why is it of crucial importance in the study of memory?

Memory may be studied in several different ways, with or without direct reference to the underlying biological structure. For example, subjects can be presented with some information and then, at a later stage, tested for their recall. In this way, we can investigate the time parameters relating to memory. Figure 4.2 shows a result obtained in this way, using human subjects. A subject is presented with a compound of three consonants (e.g. BJD), forming what is known as a *nonsense syllable*. Following an interval of time, the subject is asked to recall the item. If the subject is prevented from rehearsing the syllable during the interval, by being given a competing task, performance deteriorates quite rapidly. This indicates a rapid decay

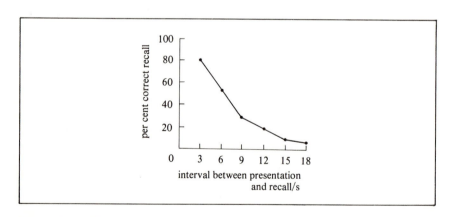

Figure 4.2 The deterioration in the ability to recall a nonsense syllable as a function of time that elapses following its presentation, when rehearsal is thwarted.

(Source: SD286, Module C2.)

of the memory trace. The memory trace seems to be in a fragile form at first. Of course, if one were to be exposed several times to the same nonsense syllable, or allowed to rehearse it, then one's ability to recall it would improve.

SAQ 44
In figure 4.2, at what delay interval has memory deteriorated to 50 per cent of its original value?

Let us now consider the possible neurophysiological bases of memory. A common assumption is that a given memory is embodied, for at least some of the time, in a pattern of activity in a particular *population* of nerve cells forming a circuit. In other words, presentation of a stimulus activates a particular circuit of neurons. (Recall the discussion of Penfield's experiments on stimulating the cortex and obtaining memory recall, described in Section 1.6). Even if such an idea later proves to be over-simple, it provides a useful starting point. Examine Figure 4.3. Presentation of a particular stimulus that activates neuron 1 might cause the circuit of nerve cells formed by neurons 2, 3, 4 and 5 to *reverberate* with electrical activity. Such reverberating activity in a specific circuit would, for as long as it lasted, embody the physical basis of the memory. Reverberation would fade with time, and so, correspondingly, would the ability to recall the stimulus, unless some other, less fragile storage medium were to be recruited. In such terms, *recall* of a memory is thought to be associated with reactivation of the same circuit that originally coded the memory (Rose, 1984).

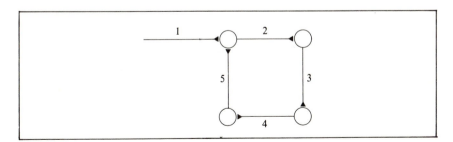

Figure 4.3   A simplified model of a circuit of neurons forming the physical basis of a memory. Suppose neuron 1 is stimulated by incoming information. This sets the circuit formed by cells 2, 3, 4 and 5 reverberating. (Source: SD286, Module C2.)

At certain periods, memory is particularly vulnerable to disruption by extraneous factors (e.g. electric shock, trauma). For example, immediately after the arrival of new information in the brain, its memory trace can relatively easily be disrupted. This leads some theorists to suppose that memory for new information is held first in a fragile store, and then, assuming it is retained at all, transferred over time into a more robust storage form. Such a process is termed *consolidation*.

A slightly different model of memory is one in which incoming information is immediately assimilated into a durable form, but *access* to this memory is open to disruption at particular stages. In other words, in the latter model, following a disruption, memory is still present in some form, but *recall* is impaired (Lewis, 1978). In the more traditional model, the memory itself is wiped out by the disturbing factor. Note that each model agrees that at certain times memory is particularly vulnerable. There is a rich body of evidence on the conditions under which memory is open to disruption.

Traumatic interference with the brain (e.g. a blow to the head in a traffic accident) often disrupts memory. Following such trauma, on regaining consciousness, a patient might be unable to remember the events immediately before the accident. Such loss of memory for events preceding trauma is known as *retrograde amnesia*. Electric shocks to the brain can also have a disruptive effect on memory. It is assumed that any trace held in the form of electrical activity in specific circuits is masked by the trauma.

SAQ 45
Does the existence of the phenomenon of retrograde amnesia support a model in which (1) memory is at first stored in a fragile form and then consolidated or (2) a durable memory is formed immediately, but retrieval is impaired?

Retrograde amnesia sometimes exhibits what is known as *shrinkage*. Memories which, immediately after the trauma, appear to be lost, will emerge over a period of weeks. Such memories were clearly present in some form throughout but were inaccessible. This phenomenon tends to support a model in which memory impairment is essentially a recall impairment.

Key Notes 4.4

1. At some stage, memory is believed to be encoded in the form

of electrical activity in circuits of neurons. Such reverberating activity constitutes the physical basis of memory.

2. Following exposure to a new stimulus, the memory of that stimulus is open to disruption. Such disruption could reflect either the loss of the memory or interference with its recall.

4.5   Structural Change and Biochemistry

Diagnostic Questions for Section 4.5

1. What aspect of memory leads us to suppose that a structural change is involved?
2. In looking for a structural change, why focus upon protein synthesis?

On the one hand, memory appears at times to be fragile and open to disruption (as discussed in the last section). It is often suggested that such fragility is the result of the embodiment of memory in a pattern of electrical activity in specific circuits. The trace tends to die out as a function of time or can be obliterated by extraneous factors. On the other hand, we must account for the impressive durability and length of retention of some of our memories (in my case, a vivid recall of my first day at school!). This implies a durable physical embodiment. It is widely assumed that this durable medium takes the form of a *structural change* in the brain; that is to say, after a memory has been firmly consolidated, the brain has, at certain sites, changed its structure (relative to its state prior to such consolidation).

Researchers have been led to the *synapse* as the most likely location at which structural change embodying memory occurs. Recall at this stage the account of habituation given in Module 3 (see pp. 43–51), as a simple example of where a memory is encoded at the synaptic level. The synapse is the point of contact between two neurons, and we know that synapses can become stronger or weaker (Rose, 1976, 1981). By 'strengthening' a synapse, one means that a given amount of activity in the presynaptic cell has a greater activity in the postsynaptic cell. This could be caused by, for example, a growth in the surface area of the synapse or a closing of the distance of the synaptic cleft. (Recall that in *Aplysia* synaptic efficiency was increased by an opening of calcium channels, though how general this mechanism is, remains unknown.) Therefore, theorists hypothesize that the long-term physical embodiment or memory is a change in synaptic structure (Hebb, 1949; Rose, 1984).

How might one investigate possible structural changes that occur during the course of learning? The actual practical problems involved are formidable (Rose, 1984), but attempts have been made, based upon the following logic. The major building blocks of cell structure are *proteins*, and therefore attention has been directed at them. Throughout the body, there occurs a permanent background level of breakdown and reconstruction of proteins. Suppose that, during learning, new synaptic structures are formed from protein at particular sites in the brain. Such structures might, in principle, involve enlargements of existing synapses or the formation of completely new synapses. One might be able to detect a localized increase in the rate at which proteins are being involved in such construction, known as *protein synthesis*. The increase would be relative to the normal background level of protein synthesis.

Amino acids are the chemical precursors of protein (i.e. they form the building blocks for proteins). Researchers have tried injecting radioactively labelled amino acids (i.e. a sample of amino acids tagged with an identifiable marker) at the time of learning. They have then measured the rate of assimilation of the tagged amino acid into protein structures at local brain sites. Experimenters have indeed found an increase in protein synthesis occurring at the time of learning (Rose, 1984). Hence, on a biochemical level, we are led to postulate that memory is encoded in the physical (protein) structures of the brain's synapses.

SAQ 46
According to the notion that memory is encoded in synaptic structures, what would be the predicted effect of injecting before, or during, training, substances that block protein synthesis?

The model of memory that is based upon structural changes at synapses being the long-term physical embodiment needs to be carefully fitted into a broader context. We have discussed the notion that memory is at first held in the relatively fragile form of the electrical activity in certain circuits of neurons. One possibility that needs to be investigated is that repeated stimulation of a given population of neurons in a circuit leads to structural changes in the synaptic connections between these neurons. This would give the particular population of neurons a privileged status, meaning that contact between the cells is facilitated by the strengthening of certain synapses. If such a process were to be taking place, then the implication is that we ought not to draw a dichotomy between memory being in the form of *either* reverberation in certain circuits *or* a structural change. Rather, we should see these as two aspects of the same phenomenon. That is to say, initially the electrical activity would be assumed to play a role in moulding synapses; however, once memory is encoded in the form of structural changes, it might well be that reactivation of the pattern of reverberating cells is more easy to achieve.

It is appropriate to return now to the general theme of this book: levels of analysis. In learning and memory, as in other domains of brain and behaviour, we are dealing with the properties of complex systems. Suppose we observe that the learning of a given task is accompanied by a particular localized change in synaptic structures. Controls for general effects of exposure to the learning situation have been run, and we are sure our effects are specific to the given learning task. In a sense, such a change would indeed form the physical embodiment of the memory in question. However, it is only meaningful to refer to such a change in these terms when we place the change into the broader context of the neural networks of which these synapses form components. An analogy can vividly illustrate the issue. Suppose we were to claim that a gramophone record of Vivaldi constitutes a memory of Vivaldi's music. Indeed, the grooves do, in a sense, represent a durable physical embodiment of a memory of Vivaldi. However, in making such a claim, we implicitly assume the existence of a larger system of gramophone plus disc, in which there are clearly defined rules for translation between groove and input to the speaker. To someone without such a complete system, the disc would in no meaningful sense constitute a memory. To all but the technical expert a disc of Vivaldi looks much the same as one by, say, The Four Freshmen or Michael Jackson. In other words, the findings of the biochemist need to be interpreted in terms of the whole animal locked into an interaction with its environment.

Key Notes 4.5

1. The durability of memory leads us to suppose that a structural change in the brain is involved. A change in synaptic connections between cells is considered to be the most likely long-term embodiment.
2. It is widely assumed that the holding of memory in a relatively fragile form tends to create structural changes that transcribe the memory into a more durable form.
3. For a given memory, possibly the synaptic connections between cells are strengthened in such a way as to facilitate activity in those circuits that initially held the memory (in its more fragile form). Thus there might be a kind of interdependence between

two aspects of the same memory: dynamic and structural aspects.

4. Protein synthesis is assumed to form the biochemical base of synaptic restructuring, and increased rates of synthesis have been observed at the time of learning.

Reading Guide

Greene, J. and Hicks, C. (1984) *Basic Cognitive Processes*, Milton Keynes, Open University Press.

Halliday, T. R. and Slater, P. J. B. (1983) *Animal Behaviour*, Oxford, Blackwell Scientific Publications, Vol. 3.

Open University *SD286, Biology, Brain and Behaviour*, Module C2, Milton Keynes, Open University Educational Enterprises.

Rose, S. P. R. (1981) 'What should a biochemistry of learning and memory be about?', *Neuroscience*, 6811–21.

—— (1984) 'Strategies in studying the cell biology of learning and memory', in L. R. Squire and N. Butters (eds.), *Neuropsychology of Memory*, New York, Guildford Press, pp. 547–54.

5   Motivation Module

Link from Learning and Memory to Motivation

The present module has a lot in common with the last. We are
dealing with a phenomenon whose neural embodiment lies in the
central nervous system: motivation. As with learning and memory,
motivation is a phenomenon that is studied at various levels by
different investigators.

General Diagnostic Questions for Motivation

1. Why do we need to consider both internal and external factors
   in motivation? (Sect. 5.1)
2. What is the relationship between regulation and motivation?
   (Sect. 5.2.)
3. In terms of motivation, compare and contrast ingestive
   behaviours and sexual behaviour. (Sect. 5.3)
4. Under what conditions might a motivational system be said to
   be in a situation of competition? (Sect. 5.4)

5.1   Definitions and Levels of Investigation

Diagnostic Questions for Section 5.1

1. What is meant by saying that motivation is goal-directed?
2. Why does the concept of drive lend itself better to hunger than
   to exploration?
3. How might one construct an index of thirst-drive?

Motivation is a topic involving different disciplines, aspects and
approaches. It concerns the complex decision-making processes that
move an animal in a particular direction towards a goal. The study
of such behaviours as feeding, drinking, sex and exploration comes
under the heading of motivation. As with other topics, we need to
simplify what is inherently complex. In investigating an individual
motivational system, such as feeding, a researcher would normally
attempt to minimize any influence on feeding arising from other
motivations, such as sex. Experimental conditions would be stand-
ardized in order to hold constant those factors arising outside the

feeding system. Water would be made available *ad lib.* so that no interacting thirst signal would be expected to arise. In addition, male rats would normally be used, to avoid problems of variations accompanying the female hormonal oestrous cycle.

A line of research and theory-building somewhat different to that of looking in detail at individual systems, is to consider the properties that various systems termed 'motivational' have in common. In other words, we need to consider what is, and what is not, a motivational system. How do individual motivational systems interact with each other? Such considerations lead the investigator to consider the animal's decision-making processes. For example, an animal might be deprived of both food and water for a period of time, and then placed in the presence of both food and water. In this way, two systems would be put in competition.

The two approaches to motivation just described have traditionally occupied different research disciplines and their associated levels of analysis. Physiological psychologists, neurophysiologists and pharmacologists have had a prime interest in investigating the biological roots of individual systems. For example, the questions asked include: how do sex hormones mediate their effect on the central nervous system? Investigators of behavioural decision-making, coming mainly from ethology, have tended to take for granted the biological bases of individual systems and look for behavioural properties arising from these systems, often when several systems are in interaction.

How might we attempt to define what is meant by a motivational system? Consideration of the common properties of what we normally term 'motivational systems' has lead some theorists to the notion of *goal-direction* (Epstein, 1982; Toates, 1986). Each motivational system can take responsibility for moving an animal towards a goal appropriate to that particular system. For example, the rat pressing a lever in a Skinner-box for food reward is said to be showing evidence of motivation. Its behaviour is directed towards the goal of attaining food. A rat in a state of food deprivation can use a variety of means to attain such a goal; for example, barpressing, running a maze or foraging in a natural environment. On gaining food, the particular form of goal-directed behaviour ceases, and the rat proceeds to ingest the food. Such goal-direction can be seen as a holistic property (see Module 1) of the whole system of rat and environment.

A further feature of motivational systems, which to some authors is the definitive one, is that under the direction of such a system the tendency to express a particular behaviour *fluctuates*. It does so in a way that is governed by the animal's *internal state*, and it is biologically appropriate. The meaning of this can be illustrated by considering that an animal that is low in energy will be particularly likely to seek and ingest food. After substantial ingestion it might then ignore the same food. In the case of sex, the responsiveness of the female often fluctuates as a function of her internal hormonal state. The hormonal (oestrous) cycle is such that sexual behaviour tends to be most strongly aroused at times when fertilization is possible. This follows logically, of course, from evolutionary considerations.

SAQ 47
How does the strength of the internal factor involved in the motivational system determining water ingestion fluctuate? What internal factor would you suggest underlies the fluctuations?

It can be useful to attempt to place motivational systems into comparison with other biological systems. In the case of a reflex, such as the light reflex of the eye's pupil, or the knee-jerk reflex, a given stimulus produces a given response, with no mediating internal state that fluctuates. As a first provisional criterion of what is, and is not, a motivational system, such a distinction can be useful.

Not only does motivation fluctuate with internal states but it also changes as a function of the external stimulus. For example, a particularly palatable food might stimulate feeding in an animal that is otherwise showing satiety. A sexually solicitous and responsive female might strongly attract a male, whereas one that is less active might provoke only slight signs of interest from the male. In other words, we need to take account of both internal and external factors in considering motivation.

Sometimes the term *drive* is used to refer to the internal contribution to motivation and *incentive* to the external. An animal deprived of food for twenty-four hours might be said to have a higher hunger-drive than one deprived for three hours. A sugar-coated biscuit would be described as having a higher incentive value for a rat than one adulterated with quinine. Such usage of terms might seem quite logical, but unfortunately the words often generate more heat than light. This is basically for two reasons. Drive and incentive in combination determine motivation. The question is: how do they interact? Simple rules of combination were proposed, such as motivation equals drive multiplied by incentive. Such rules were shown to be inadequate in some situations, which suggested the need for more complex rules. Second, it was assumed that drive would have common properties that would make the concept equally applicable to, say, hunger and exploration. However, differences between motivations soon appeared.

It is not too difficult to envisage a hunger- or thirst-drive, something that increases in parallel with depletion of energy or water. Clearly, internal physiological changes are involved. Other motivational systems lend themselves much less well to the drive notion. For example, how might we envisage an exploratory drive? No obvious physiological change is involved as a function of deprivation. There is not necessarily an increase in the tendency to explore as a function of time spent not exploring. Yet some animals show a strong tendency to explore their environments. Similarly, depriving an animal of the opportunity to fight does not appear to lead to the accumulation of an 'aggression drive', just bursting to be released. For these reasons, amongst others, attempts to apply a generic explanatory drive notion to all such motivational systems are now much less common.

In particular cases, attempts have been made to construct a quantitative *index* of an animal's drive level. For example, as the period of prior water deprivation increases, a rat will drink more when water is subsequently made available. Thus we can derive an index in terms of quantity drunk. Another possible index of thirst-drive is the amount of quinine that the rat is prepared to tolerate in its drinking water. As time of deprivation goes up, so the rat becomes less discriminating. Third, as deprivation increases, so does the vigour with which an animal will perform an instrumental task, such as bar-pressing in a Skinner-box (see Module 4), to gain the missing commodity. However, unfortunately for those who like parsimony, the relationship between deprivation and these three indices is by no means a simple one. There is a general trend for the three measures to increase with deprivation, but at times one of them can change without the others. For example, increasing the physiological stimulus to drink might increase the *amount* drunk when water is made freely available but not change the rat's willingness to bar-press to obtain water. In other words, incentives and cues that predict such incentives (e.g. the lever in the Skinner-box) form complex interactions with internal states, as revealed in indices of motivation.

Key Notes 5.1

1. We can choose to study an individual system while attempting to minimize the influence of other variables. For other

purposes, we need to look at the outcome of the interactions between more than one motivational system.

2. A motivational system is one in which behaviour is directed towards the attainment of a goal. Such behaviour takes cognizance of internal factors (e.g. energy or hormone levels).

3. The internal factor in motivation is sometimes termed 'drive' and the external factor termed 'incentive'.

5.2   Ingestive Behaviour

Diagnostic Questions for Section 5.2

1. What do we know about the biological roots of drinking motivation?
2. What is meant by the terms 'negative feedback', 'positive feedback' and 'set-point'?
3. Why do we believe short-term feedback loops to be part of the systems of feeding and drinking?

The body consists of a multitude of various cells (see Module 1)—for example, nerve cells (neurons), skin and kidney cells—and all of these require a supply of energy in order to perform their different functions. This energy is derived from ingested food. The cells contain a large percentage of water (Module 2), and the spaces betweeen the cells are filled with water. Of course, the blood also has a large water content. Water is lost from the body as urine, sweat and perspiration. Water is gained, in part, from ingested food, but normally it is derived mainly from drinking.

Certain of the variables of the internal environment of the body, such as water, glucose level and temperature, are maintained within fairly close limits. If such a variable departs significantly from its optimal level, the body takes corrective action to return it to normal. For example, in humans, an increase in body temperature to above normal elicits sweating. This maintenance of important variables at a relatively constant level and taking corrective action in response to deviations from the optimal level is known as *homeostasis*. Sometimes one finds the term *set-point* in the literature. This refers to the value of a physiological variable for which the system appears to be striving. Furthermore, if a departure from the set-point occurs, the system will take corrective action involving an exertion of effort to return to the set-point. The motivational systems of feeding and drinking form part of homeostatic systems that *regulate* nutrient and fluid levels. For example, a disturbance to the body fluids by injection of salt is followed by drinking an amount commensurate with the size of the disturbance. Conversely, force-feeding is likely to be followed by a period of abstinence from food.

A homeostatic system, in which deviation from a particular condition causes a corrective action to occur so as to tend to return the variable in question to its previous condition, is an example of a *negative feedback* system. The basic feature is that a change in an internal state is compensated for by negative feedback, so as to return the system to its original state. On the one hand, feeding and drinking motivation form essential components of negative feedback systems. On the other hand, we must always bear in mind the powerful motivational (incentive) role of palatability. At times this can appear to mask the regulatory aspect of the system (e.g. gorging on exotic cuisine). Any convincing model of motivation must attempt to integrate these two factors.

In order to exhibit homeostasis, the body must be able to detect the current level of its various internal states. Such detection then plays a role in the subsequent corrective action. Exactly where is the actual level of body water and nutrients measured? In relation to feeding and drinking as individual systems, a large amount of research effort has been devoted to trying to establish the locations and characteristics of the *detectors*.

Drinking is perhaps better understood then feeding. As an analogy to water regulation and drinking, consider the thermostat in a room. The heating effort, and hence the temperature throughout the room, depend upon the temperature detected at one particular location (a 'sample' temperature). Nonetheless, such a system is able to maintain a reasonably uniform temperature throughout the room. By analogy, researchers look for particular sites of detection of fluid states, which enable the remainder of the body to maintain its fluid state. The assumption is generally made that the level of fluid at such a site is translated into the activity level of a neuron (or neurons). Possibly, the frequency of action potentials yields a measure of fluid state at the site of the transducer. One major focus of attention in the search for such a transducer has been in the brain region known as the *hypothalamus*. A hypothalamic cell would signal its state of dehydration, possibly by generating action potentials. These would then play a role in the decision to drink. Certainly electrical and chemical stimulation of this brain region can lead to the arousal of drinking. In the case of feeding, in recent years considerable interest has focused upon the *liver* as a possible site at which the body's nutrient state is monitored. Any signal originating at the liver would be transmitted to the brain, where behavioural decision-making is integrated.

The determinants of feeding and drinking are many, particularly in a natural environment. Clearly, negative feedback is an essential aspect of such systems, since feeding and drinking are particularly likely to occur at times of relative depletion. We have noted the powerful role of palatability. Ease of availability is another factor; a readily available food might be eaten in larger amounts than one for which great effort must be exerted. A simple laboratory cage with food of a fixed quality available *ad lib*. provides a means of holding the external factors of incentive quality and availability constant. In such an artificially simple environment we can more easily observe the role of the internal factor. Given such an environment, one can to some extent predict when a rat will feed or drink, based upon the time elapsing since the last meal or drink (LeMagnen, 1985).

The onset of a particular meal or drink is determined by a combination of the appropriate external incentive that is available and the level of the internal physiological variable. Given this assumption, what *terminates* meals and drinks? Before we attempt to answer this, let us consider more closely what is involved in drinking and the animal's fluid state. Water enters the mouth, passes down the oesophagus and into the stomach. It then passes into the intestine, where it is absorbed across the intestinal wall into the blood. In effect, it is then circulated by the blood and permeates the various cells of the body.

We have supposed that drinking is aroused by a fall in the level of water at a particular site in the brain. It can be demonstrated that, following the onset of drinking, it requires a substantial amount of time before the water level at such brain sites returns to normal (Toates and Oatley, 1970). However, following a period of prior deprivation, animals such as rats and dogs drink very rapidly and generally terminate their drink after having taken an amount commensurate with the size of their deficit. This implies that, at the time of terminating the drink, the original excitatory stimulus at the detector site still exists, at least in part. So, what mechanism causes them to stop drinking? We believe that there are inhibitory pathways running from the mouth and stomach. These provide what is known as *short-term feedback loops*. Their activation by water passing the mouth and in the stomach helps to switch drinking off. The expression 'short term' refers to the fact that this inhibition lasts only for a while. However, it is of sufficient duration to restrain drinking until restoration of body-fluid state at the detector site in the brain occurs.

SAQ 48
Suppose in response to a particular stimulus a rat drinks a certain amount. Then imagine that we find a way of eliminating its short-term inhibitory feedback loops. What might be the response of the animal to the same drinking stimulus?

A very similar argument to that just developed can be applied to feeding. In some species, a meal is finished before appreciable amounts of digested material have been absorbed across the intestine wall, and therefore before the internal energy state signal can be corrected. This indicates the need for short-term inhibitory pathways as part of the feeding system. However, it is more difficult here to speak with the same confidence as for drinking, since we still don't know the location of the sensor that monitors nutrient levels.

Key Notes 5.2

1. Feeding and drinking are behavioural means of regulating the state of the animal's internal environment. These behaviours form part of homeostatic motivational systems that exhibit negative feedback.
2. Transducers detect the level of fluid and nutrients somewhere within the system, and the signals arising thereby play a crucial role in the motivation to drink and feed.
3. In some species, short-term feedback loops play an important role in terminating drinking and feeding.

5.3 Sexual Behaviour

Diagnostic Questions for Section 5.3

1. What is the significance of the oestrus cycle so far as female sexual motivation is concerned?
2. What is the role of testosterone in male sexual behaviour?

Comparing sex with the ingestive systems of feeding and drinking yields some important similarities and differences. Looking at the function that these systems serve, we immediately see a crucial difference. In the prolonged absence of food or water, the metabolic disturbance is fatal: feeding and drinking serve *individual* survival. By contrast, sexual behaviour does not play any such obvious role in individual survival. Rather, it is concerned with reproduction, or, in terms popular at the moment, *gene perpetuation* (see Sect. 1.3). However, this difference in function should not allow important similarities in causal mechanisms to be missed.

Sexual motivation is aroused by a combination of external and internal factors in a manner similar to ingestive behaviour. In the case of sex, the external factor or 'incentive' is usually a *conspecific* (an animal of the same species) of the opposite sex. The partner can be more or less arousing depending upon its hormonal state and behaviour. What are the determinants of the internal factor? In the male, the time elapsing since ejaculation ('deprivation period') plays a vital role. Ejaculation (or a series of ejaculations) desensitizes the motivational system. Sex hormones also play a vital role.

In the case of the female of some species, the effect of hormones may well mask any deprivation effect that is present; that is, female responsiveness to the male fluctuates with the level of *oestrogen* and *progesterone* in the blood. The level of these hormones oscillates in the form of a cycle, known as the *oestrus cycle*. In the case of the female rat, the period of this cycle is about four days.

It is believed that sex hormones are taken up by neurons in the circuits underlying sexual motivation. On so doing, the neurons change their characteristics. For example, it might be very easy to cause them to generate action potentials following such take up of hormones. Whatever the exact mechanism, hormones are said to *sensitize* the animal to sexual arousal. The female will then take active steps to mate with the male and respond positively to the male's mating attempts.

For the male rat, on attaining adulthood the hormone levels remain relatively constant, in the sense of not showing pronounced cycles. *Testosterone* is a hormone that plays a key role in male sexual behaviour. Loss of this hormone, through, for example, castration usually leads to a decline in sexual responsiveness. Artificial restoration of hormonal level usually restores sexual arousability.

In some species, *novelty*, the replacement of a familiar partner by an unfamiliar one, causes a relatively high level of sexual motivation. This phenomenon has come to be termed the *Coolidge effect*. The term derives from the former US president of that name. It is said that during a visit to a poultry station, the president and first lady were taken around the station in two different groups. First, Mrs Coolidge was shown a cockerel that was particularly active, and asked 'does he perform like that all day?' The technician answered that this was indeed the case. Mrs Coolidge requested that the cockerel should be pointed out to President Coolidge when the president reached this part of the visit. Some time later, the president arrived and the technician mentioned the wish of Mrs Coolidge that he should be shown the male of such a high libido. President Coolidge posed the question 'but do they regularly change the female?'. The technician replied 'yes', to which president Coolidge added 'well, don't forget to tell that to Mrs Coolidge!'.

In a functional sense, to what extent, if any, an otherwise satiated member of a particular species can be rearoused by a change of partner depends upon the whole mating and reproduction system of the species in question.

Key Notes 5.3

1. Sexual behaviour serves the function of reproduction rather than individual survival through regulation.
2. As with ingestive behaviours, sexual motivation arises from a combination of internal and external factors.
3. Internal state depends upon hormone level and deprivation.

5.4 Interactions between Motivational Systems

Diagnostic Questions for Section 5.4

1. In behavioural decision-making, why do we invoke the notion of *inhibition*?
2. Under what circumstances might an animal fail to observe the needs of an individual system?

Animals need to make decisions. We can appreciate this when we consider the many activities that an animal in the wild has to perform. It must eat, drink, groom, mate, sleep and, at the same time, avoid being eaten by a predator and defend its resources against competitors. A large number of activities must be fitted into the available time in order for the animal to function in anything like an optimal way.

The necessary internal and external factors for more than one motivation might be simultaneously present, and yet the animal might be able to pursue only one goal at a time. For example, a rat might be simultaneously deprived of food and water over a period of time and then placed in the start-box of a T-maze. The arm to the left would contain food and that to the right contain water. Having experienced this maze, the rat is obviously confronted with a choice at the junction. Unlike the proverbial ass that died of starvation midway between two bundles of hay, animals generally rather quickly resolve such decisions and unambiguously commit themselves to one or other goal. Suppose tendencies to turn left and right exist simultaneously, but that the rat takes the left turn towards food. We assume that, at some level in the nervous system, *inhibition* is exerted from the feeding (left turn) tendency to the drinking (right turn) tendency. This allows the rat to respond to the excitation underlying the feeding tendency, and to inhibit any simultaneous tendency to carry out a competing activity.

Figure 5.1 shows the result obtained from the study of a hen during incubation of her eggs. Note the loss of body weight over the period of incubation. Despite the fact that food is available at a distance of only 50 cm from her nest, she eats relatively little. One possible explanation might be that the motivational system of incubation exerts an inhibition upon that of feeding. Other possible modes of interaction can be envisaged, but it is clear that one cannot explain the bird's feeding behaviour simply by looking at events in the energy-regulation/feeding system. It is necessary to look at interactions of this system with other systems, in this case interactions between feeding and incubation. Note that earlier, on examining individual systems, we deliberately tried to minimize the role of interactions.

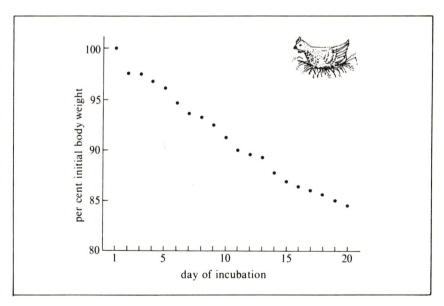

Figure 5.1   The change in weight of a hen over the period of incubation.
(Source: SD286, Module C4.)

Looking at the incubation study from a functional point of view, one can appreciate that the behavioural strategy maximizes reproductive chances. By remaining most of the time with the eggs, the hen minimizes the risk of either the eggs chilling or their being snatched by a predator. In such a situation of behavioural choice, an animal might have to sacrifice, to some extent, the interests of a single system (in this case, feeding/energy regulation) in the interests of a 'higher goal', reproductive success. Of course, this in no sense diminishes the importance of energy regulation. Circumstances permitting, it would be to the hen's advantage to return to its optimal body weight.

As we noted earlier, where choices have to be made, they are usually done rapidly with a minimum of ambivalence. However, sometimes choices do appear to be accompanied by external indices of what might be termed *motivational conflict*. For example, a given stimulus might have a tendency to elicit two incompatible courses of action. For the male, a female animal can arouse simultaneous tendencies to attack and to mate. In such a situation, animals sometimes show behaviour that appears irrelevant to either course of action. Thus, in the middle of conflict, when the obvious two courses of action are to flee or fight, a bird might start to preen itself. Such apparently irrelevant actions are sometimes termed *displacement activities*. One should be cautious in using the expression 'irrelevant' to describe such behaviour. It might indeed turn out to be so, but it might also serve a function that is at present not apparent to researchers.

Key Notes 5.4

1. Normally animals are confronted with the need to make decisions. One object or course of action can only be pursued at the expense of not doing something else.
2. Where external and internal factors for two motivational systems exist simultaneously, inhibition will be exerted from one system to the other.
3. Survival of the whole animal and its reproductive success often dictate that an animal should, to a limited extent, sacrifice the interests of one motivational system in order to benefit one having a higher priority at the time concerned.
4. Decision-making is usually done rapidly and efficiently. However, it is also possible to identify situations in which the animal appears ambivalent as to which course to pursue. In such a situation, it sometimes exhibits behaviour that appears irrele-

vant to the obvious goals of the situation. Such a behaviour is termed a 'displacement activity'.

Reading Guide

Open University *SD286, Biology, Brain and Behaviour*, Module C4, Milton Keynes, Open University Educational Enterprises.

Toates, F. M. (1980) *Animal Behaviour: A Systems Approach*, Chichester, Wiley.

—— (1986) *Motivational Systems*, Cambridge, Cambridge University Press.

6   Theoretical Issues Module

Link from Motivation to Theoretical Issues

So far, the modules have developed the idea of levels of explanation. However, despite the difference in levels, we have remained within a certain well-defined framework. We have looked at biology and behaviour in the traditional scientific way of making empirical observations and then attempting to fit theories and models to them. We have not questioned the broader implications of the topics under discussion; for example, in social, ethical and political life. This chapter briefly looks at some of these broader theoretical implications.

Ideas generated in the behavioural and brain sciences are of profound importance to the society in which we live. To a considerable extent, our culture reflects views on the determinants of behaviour and the nature of brain and mind. The assumptions that we make concerning the thoughts and actions of ourselves and others critically depend upon the 'models' and analogies that we employ to describe brain and behaviour. A good example of an issue of basic social relevance, in which naive biology is often applied, is that of the role of genes and environment (nature and nurture) in the determination of behaviour. Unfortunately, space precludes a discussion of this issue here.

General Diagnostic Questions for Theoretical Issues

1. In terms of identity theory, what is the relationship between mind events and brain events? (Sect. 6.1)
2. What is revealed by damage to the brain? (Sect. 6.2)
3. What is the central theme of Skinnerian psychology? (Sect. 6.3.)

6.1   Mind and Brain

Diagnostic Questions for Section 6.1

1. What is meant by the expression 'dualism'?
2. In what way does identity theory differ from the view that mind is an epiphenomenon of brain?

Let us consider two domains of discourse. The first is that of the nervous system, made up of neurons, neurotransmitters and other things describable in physico-chemical terms. Using the electron microscope and other techniques, one can gain a fine-grained understanding of the physical structure of the cells that make up this system. With the aid of models, and an understanding of how systems of nerve cells might function, we can show how certain properties, such as habituation, emerge. We can see how some aspects of experience, such as pain, learning and motivation, might, in a limited event, be explained in terms of the nervous system. The second domain of discourse to be considered is that of our conscious *being* in the world. The thoughts, joys, hopes, fears, and so on, that we experience as something private, form the subject matter of this second domain. It is impossible to capture in simple unambiguous terms what is meant by this personal conscious state, but at least it would seem a reasonable assumption that this is a state that we share with other human beings. The nature of the relationship between these two domains is one that has occupied the attention of philosophers, scientists and theologians. Doubtless, it will continue to do so. For obvious reasons, students of brain and behaviour are attracted to this discussion. However, what these sciences have to offer the debate will probably not give anyone that pleasant feeling of resolution, like finding a long-awaited answer in a crossword. At least, though, we can probably couch the discussion in somewhat more useful terms with the assistance of an understanding of brain and behaviour.

Perhaps the most influential statement to have been made on the nature of the relationship between brain and mind was that of the French philosopher, René Descartes. His notion of the relationship is termed *dualism*. Basically, Descartes envisaged two distinct kinds of 'stuff': mind and body. In addition to their physical bodies, humans were endowed with 'mind-stuff'. This is something of spiritual, non-material qualities, in distinction to physical matter. Animals ('brutes') had only the physical part. Despite being two fundamentally different sorts of 'stuff', according to Descartes, mind and brain can *interact*. The mind is able to influence the physical body. Thus, by volition, one can move muscles and behave. This might be termed 'mind over matter'.

A somewhat different view of brain and mind, espoused originally by T. Huxley, is known as *epiphenomenalism*. According to this view, brain and mind refer to two sets of events running in parallel. For every brain event, there is a corresponding mind event. However, the relationship is *unilateral*: the brain events cause the corresponding mind events. The mind events are unable to exert an influence on the brain events. The brain is the instigator of action, and the mind is a passive translation of the brain events. One might like to term this 'matter over mind'.

SAQ 49
In what essential respect does the model of mind as an epipheno-menon differ from Descartes' dualism?

A simple analogy might enlighten the model. Consider, during the Second World War, a British spy monitoring the discussion at German High Command, and providing a simultaneous translation into English. The two events, English and German, run in parallel. Although very different, rules of translation exist between the two. However, only the German words influence the decision-making of the High Command and their instigation of action. The English words would simply be the passenger (or 'epiphenomenon') of the German words.

SAQ 50
Suppose we assume that mind is an epiphenomenon of brain. What might such a belief lead to, in terms of attaching status and import-ance to the study of mind and brain?

Perhaps the view of brain and mind most widely accepted at the moment, at least amongst behavioural scientists, is that of *identity theory* (e.g. Rose, 1976, 1981). If we needed to employ an expression to summarize this, we might say that 'mind equals matter', though even that might not fully capture the essence of identity theory. In the view of identity theorists, brain events and mental events are, in a sense, identical. By this is meant that there is a single event, but

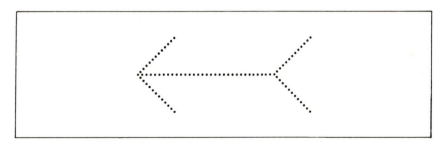

Figure 6.1   Arrow formed from eighty dots.

two different languages that can be used to describe it. Neither brain language nor mind language is superior. We can employ either account, according to the purpose of our exposition. For a simple analogy, look at Figure 6.1. Is this an arrow or eighty dots? Clearly, the very same thing can be described in either way. There is not an arrow and, *in addition*, eighty dots. The arrow *is* the eighty dots, expressed in other words and with another purpose in mind. In a similar way, there is not a mental domain that is in any meaningful sense distinct from a neurophysiological domain. By analogy, the arrow does not have an embodiment beyond the dots.

SAQ 51
Suppose Jones were to argue that humans are motivated to maximize subjective sensory pleasure. Brown disputes this, saying that they are motivated to maximize the electrical activity of certain neurons in the hypothalamus. What might an identity theorist say to Jones and Brown?

The variety of identity theory proposed by Rose stands in opposition to the kind of naive reductionism that believes that the duty of behavioural science is to reduce phenomena to a lower level. Such reductionism would see the goal of behavioural science to be the achievement of an account in biochemical terms. This would then supercede the psychological account, which could be discarded. According to Rose (1976, 1981, 1984), the duty of behavioural science is not to attempt to collapse mental events into ones at a lower level, but to find the *rules of translation* between mental and brain events. In some ways, this is analogous to searching for the rules of translation between, say, English and French.

SAQ 52
Suppose Bill said that he hit Jack because Jack made him angry? What status would such a claim have to a non-reductionist identity theorist? How would its status compare to an explanation in terms of brain events occurring at the time of the assault?

SAQ 53
According to (1) the view of mind as an epiphenomenon and (2) identity theory, does the mental state of joy cause the brain state with which it is associated?

An identity theory of the kind described here has something clear to say about so-called *psychosomatic illness*. It is said that a bodily illness can be caused by psychological events. Normal usage of this term implies that something within a psychological domain can influence physical events in the body. Were the expression to mean simply that such phenomena as fear, stress and depression can exert influences in the body, no offence would be done to an identity theorist. However, the implicit assumption is usually made that the cause is *purely* psychological, meaning that no physical correlates exist for the causal agent. Identity theory would reject such dualism, proposing instead that for every psychological cause there exists a brain (i.e. physical, or somatic) correlate. That is to say, nothing can exist 'only in the mind'.

A way of looking at the mind that is rather different to the approaches so far described, but is not necessarily incompatible with any of them, is in terms of emergent properties (described in Module 1). What might we mean by saying that the mind is an emergent property? We noted earlier that, when components are put together in systems, complex properties can emerge. The emergent phenomenon need in no way be evident in the performance characteristics of individual components of the system (see Module 1). One might argue that the phenomena of conscious life emerge at a certain complexity of brain structure. Thus it might be the case that consciousness *suddenly* appears at a certain level of complexity. If this were so, it would be a mistake to consider a scale of consciousness ranging from, say, the fly (consciousness absent), through the rat (partial conscious state) to humans (full consciousness).

Key Notes 6.1

1. Various notions of the relationship between mental events and brain events have been proposed (e.g. dualism).
2. One of the more popular models these days is identity theory, in which brain events and mental events are considered to be identical. Thus physical and mental languages can be seen as two different ways of describing the same thing.

6.2   Some Issues Raised by Reductionism

Diagnostic Questions for Section 6.2

1. What is revealed by the removal of a component of a system?

2. Is brain science ideologically neutral?
3. Does the co-existence of an abnormal biochemical state in the brain and abnormal behaviour demonstrate a causal connection?

Viewed in the context of an understanding of the system of which it is a part, a knowledge of the role of an individual component can be vital. However, we need to interpret such evidence with care, since a number of pitfalls await the unwary. A simple analogy, suggested by Richard Gregory, very vividly illustrates this. Suppose that you have a transistor radio that is working perfectly. You then remove one of its component transistors, and the radio emits an intolerable howl. No one, least of all an electrical engineer, would suggest that the normal function served by this transistor is to inhibit howling. By removing a component, we reveal, not the normal function of that component, but the properties of the remaining system. The moral is that any conclusions made on the basis of damaged brains must be backed up by some kind of theory regarding the role of the damaged region in the normal and damaged brain. We cannot simply assume that what is missing in behaviour corresponds to the function of the missing region.

The pitfalls of naive reductionism can become apparent in the language that we use to describe localization of function in terms of *brain centres*. For example, Broca's area is sometimes termed a 'speech centre' and the lateral hypothalamus a 'feeding centre'. Such terminology might lead the unwary to suppose that such centres have exclusive or autonomous control over distinct behaviours. So serious is the problem that 'centre' is a word that is probably best avoided. Any behaviour, involving as it necessarily does incoming information, stored information and muscular output, will depend upon the interconnections between numerous brain regions. In a few well-worked-out cases we are able to assign particular roles to particular regions, an example being the special role of Broca's and Wernicke's areas in speech. However, such understanding is only possible in the context of knowing about the relationship between the region in question and other regions of the brain (e.g. sensory receiving areas and motor control areas). Contrary to the assumptions of *phrenology*, clearly circumscribed areas of the brain having responsibility for such human activities and character traits as stamp collecting, jealousy and sexual promiscuity simply do not exist.

The implications of reductionism extend well beyond the domain of the brain and behavioural sciences, into ethics, politics and religion. Take for example a controversy that came into particular focus in the USA in the 1960s. At the time of serious rioting in the urban ghettos of several large American cities, it was noted that only a small minority of ghetto inhabitants actually participated in such riots. Of course, rioter and non-rioter alike were subjected to the same ghetto environment, and, it was argued, this eliminated the environment as a possible explanation for the aberrant behaviour. The cause, it was argued, must lie in the head of the rioter. As a solution, it was proposed to make selective lesions to the brains of rioters.

The point is not so much whether this represents good or bad science. It might indeed be possible to thwart rioting by selective brain lesions, just as it would clearly be possible with limb amputation. What is important is that such a prescription, in locating the cause of the problem in the head of an individual, is making a political and moral statement. A non-reductionist behavioural biology might wish to see the cause of deviant behaviour residing neither in the head nor in the environment as distinct entitities, but rather as something emerging from the interactions of environment and organism. As such, an enlightened biology might lead one to emphasize the environment as a more acceptable target for change. Presumably, both food-seeking and the subjective sensation of hunger are phenomena closely associated with the brain. However, it would be a wild extrapolation from this to suggest that the answer to starvation is to be found by looking inside the brain. To do so, is to make a morally and ideologically loaded argument. It is not part of our brief to persuade the reader of the validity of any particular political philosophy, merely to point out that (1) an understanding of brain science does not necessarily offer a superior remedy for the ills of society, and (2) conclusions regarding intervention, based on brain events, will have broader social and moral implications.

Naive reductionism can also create problems in the case of a mental illness, where an excess or deficiency of a substance might be observed in the brain. The obvious temptation seems to be to see the altered chemical state as the *cause* of the deviant behaviour. Clearly, the state of the brain can be caused to change, and so can the mental states that are identical with the brain states. One can cause brain states to change by drinking alcohol or injecting heroin. In such cases, there is a temporal sequence involved. However, one cannot necessarily assume that in the case of an abnormal chemical brain state and aberrant behaviour that the latter was caused by the former. The chemical change might have been the *consequence* of the illness, or both the chemical state and the abnormal behaviour might be the consequence of some other factor.

Key Notes 6.2

1. Removal of a brain region reveals the performance of the remaining system.
2. To allocate the cause of deviant behaviour in the head of an individual can raise important ideological issues.

6.3   Beyond Freedom and Dignity?

Diagnostic Questions for Section 6.3

1. To a Skinnerian, what is the determinant of behaviour that needs to form our object of study?
2. Is Skinner a reductionist?
3. Why does the Skinnerian message generate so much passion?

The principles of learning (i.e. instrumental and classical conditioning) have been developed largely on the basis of laboratory experiments using, rats, pigeons and dogs. In some cases, humans have been employed as subjects. Can the principles of learning, developed under such circumstances, be applied to the complex problems of human society?

The most famous exponent of the view that we ought to apply to human society the principles of learning derived in the laboratory is the American behaviourist B. F. Skinner (see Module 4 for an account of experiments on conditioning). Skinner believes that although classical conditioning is a means of behavioural change, the most important means is via instrumental contingencies. Skinner was responsible for a series of experiments showing how an experimenter can *shape* the behaviour of an animal. The word 'shape' derives from an analogy with moulding clay. From an unformed lump, an object can be formed. Similarly, Skinner shows how by use of positive reinforcement a new behaviour can be shaped; for example, a pigeon can be taught ten-pin bowling by rewarding successive approximations to the desired behaviour. Skinner (1973) proposes that we should use such a technology of behavioural change to cure all the ills of society. Thus, at present, offenders are put in prison to punish undesirable behaviour. Skinner would argue that we need to focus upon rewarding desirable behaviour. Ultimately, by such means, Skinnerians envisage the creation of a Utopian society on earth, based upon mutual positive reinforcement.

The Skinnerian message generates an enormous amount of heat. To the supporters of this movement, it promises a science of behaviour that can be used to cure our ills. This would herald a new era in which punishment and the threat of punishment become extinct. To the opponents of behaviourism, to deny the notion of human freedom and freewill is to deny what is most essentially human. The idea that the behaviour of humans can be *determined* as a result of the application of planned contingencies of reinforcement is an anathema to them. In such terms, to see humans as being on a behavioural continuum with rats and pigeons is to degrade them. Some see the notion of adminstering positive reinforcement as being essentially totalitarian. Opponents of Skinner ask who is to be the Big Brother responsible for conditioning everyone else and for deciding which behaviours are desirable? Which should be extinguished by removal of reinforcement? Skinnerians reply that society already sets goals, but lacks an adequate technology of behaviour to allow these goals to be realized. For example, we abhor crime, but punish criminals rather than shaping them in new directions.

Is Skinner a reductionist? In one sense he is, but in another sense he most certainly is not. If one considers reductionism to be breaking up of a complex situation into the sum of its parts, then there might be some justification for seeing Skinner as a reductionist. He views complex behaviour, such as speaking a language, as the outcome of a series of single learned associations. Words are emitted because, in the past, in a similar situation they were followed by reinforcement. However, if, by the expression 'reductionism' we mean the tendency to explain phenomena at one level in terms of events at a lower level (see Fig. 1.1, p. 2). Skinner is not a reductionist. He makes no appeal to events at a neurophysiological level in searching for the determinants of behaviour. There are (psychological) behavioural laws, and these can, according to Skinner, be deduced from looking at the relationship between the whole organism and its environment. Of course, Skinner does not deny that the nervous system mediates between the environment and behaviour. He argues that it is in the environment that we have control over behaviour by the use of positive reinforcement, and so should focus our attention there.

Whatever your views about Skinner's approach, if we believe identity theory, his account would be simply *one* way of describing what is going on. Explanations at other levels (e.g. neurophysiology and biochemistry) would be equally viable. It all depends on the purpose to which you want to put the explanation, and you might judge it to be prudent to accept evidence from several levels.

Key Notes 6.3

1. Skinner proposes that human progress requires the implementation of a technology of behavioural change.

2. The major controlling factor in behaviour is reinforcement from the organism's environment.
3. Skinner's view that we can discard the notion of freedom in favour of a model in which behaviour is shaped by reinforcement arouses both passionate defence and opposition.
4. Most researchers in the area of brain and behaviour consider it worth attempting to describe behaviour at various levels; for example, in terms of biochemistry and neurophysiology.

Reading Guide

Blakemore, C. (1977) *Mechanics of the Mind*, Cambridge, Cambridge University Press.

Carpenter, F. (1974) *The Skinner Primer*, New York, The Free Press.

Open University *SD286, Biology, Brain and Behaviour*, Modules A, D2, D3, Milton Keynes, Open University Educational Enterprises.

Skinner, B. F. (1973) *Beyond Freedom and Dignity*, Harmondsworth, Penguin.

Rose, S. P. R. (1976) *The Conscious Brain*, Harmondsworth, Penguin.

7 Some Notes on Experimental Design

This section is designed to give you some impression of the issues involved in designing experiments in the area of brain and behaviour. Experimental design and statistical methods for analysing the significance of experimental findings are dealt with in another Open Guide to Psychology volume, *Learning to Use Statisical Tests in Psychology: A Student's Guide*, by Judith Greene and Manuela D'Oliveira, available from Open University Educational Enterprises.

A feature that is common to a large amount of research in the area of brain and behaviour is that an experimenter manipulates some aspect of the environment and then sees the consequence of this manipulation. Experimentation of this form starts with the notion that if a variable over which the experimenter has direct control (x) is manipulated, we can then observe the variable that depends upon x. Let us call it y. The variable that we, as experimenters, can manipulate directly is known as the *independent variable*. The variable that we do not have direct control over, but might be able to influence via the independent variable, is known as the *dependent variable*. These terms are best illustrated with examples. Suppose you want to investigate the effect of alcohol on a subject's self-report of euphoria or depression. You assume that this subjective state depends upon the amount of alcohol that you allow them to drink. You have direct control over the amount of alcohol that you give them, which is presented in predetermined amounts and at specified times. You than investigate their mood changes.

The quantity of alcohol administered is the independent variable—that over which you have direct control and that which you manipulate. The subject's mood is the dependent variable. You do not have direct control over this. This is the variable that is assumed to be under the influence of the independent variable. In order to get the terms straight, note that mood (dependent) is thought to be dependent upon alcohol (independent), but there is no sense in which, in this experiment, amount of alcohol given depended upon mood.

Our hypothesis might be that mood depends upon the amount of alcohol given, but of course whether there really is such a dependence can only be decided by the outcome of the experiment. It is an hypothesis that we test by experimentation. Such an hypothesis that we test is often termed the *experimental hypothesis*.

SAQ 54
With reference to Module 5, suppose we wanted to investigate the relationship between (1) hours of water deprivation in rats and (2) the amount that rats drink following deprivation when water is restored. What might be our experimental hypothesis? What would be our independent and dependent variables in such an experiment?

SAQ 55

In the experiment whose result is shown in Figure 4.2 (see p. 78), what are the independent and dependent variables?

To summarize, we make a change in an independent variable and then see what effect this has upon the dependent variable. In principle, this might sound easy, but, when we come to test experimental hypotheses, the actual procedure of experimental design is fraught with problems.

Suppose I claim to have found a substance that lowers the appetite of rats by acting on their hunger control system. Injected in small amounts, it will reliably reduce the amount of food eaten. How might we test such an hypothesis? Suppose that we observe that following a period of 12 hours food deprivation, rats reliably eat about 10 grammes of food. Then one day I inject a group of rats with the substance in question and observe that they eat nothing. Has my hypothesis that the drug suppresses hunger been verified? It might indeed have had the effect claimed, but, from the procedure as described, we could not conclude that this was necessarily so. It might be that all the rats had been taken ill in the night and would have eaten nothing in any case.

To deal with this problem we need a *control group*: a number of rats housed under identical conditions to the experimentals, but not subject to injection of the chemical. We then compare the behaviour of this control group with that of the *experimental group* consisting of the rats that we have manipulated by injecting them with the chemical. The depression of food intake seen by the experimental group might have been due to the chemical effect. However, it might be that, rather than being taken ill in the night, the experimental group of rats have a perfectly reasonable objection to being picked up and injected. This procedure might disturb them so much that they cannot eat anything for several hours after the injection. To answer this, we would need to inject our control rats in an identical fashion with a substance known to have no effect on feeding.

What we are doing essentially is to ensure that conditions for the control group are as nearly identical to those for the experimental group as we can possibly make them, with the exception of the one factor: the chosen independent variable, presence of the drug. We must start by selecting subjects for our experimental and control groups that are as similar as possible. For example, control and experimental rats need to be of the same sex, age and weight. We need to make experimental conditions identical except concerning the *one* manipulation we are studying. If a difference emerges, we can then conclude that there is a true effect of the independent variable at work. Suppose we follow a rigorously correct experimental design and find that injection of the chemical does indeed lower food intake. Our procedure enables us to eliminate factors concerned with the injection *per se* as being implicated, so we are sure that it is the chemical properties that are important.

We still need to be cautious in any interpretation of the results. We cannot assume that we have found a chemical that mimics natural satiety for food. We need to perform more tests before taking out a patent designed to cure the problems of overeating. Our experiment has not shown us how, or at what site, the drug exerts its effects. Does it act specifically upon the hunger control system, mimicking the effects of natural satiety? It might simply make the rats feel ill and would therefore depress the expression of any form of motivation. One obvious experiment would be to see whether it lowers the amount of water drunk by thirsty rats. If so, it might be having very general effects. If it does not affect other motivational systems, we might be nearer to showing a genuine appetite depressant effect.

Suppose we wish to see whether human subjects receiving electroconvulsive therapy (ECT) for serious depression improve as a result of the procedure. We take two groups of subjects: to one group (the experimental group) we give ECT and, to the other group (the control group) we do not give ECT. Subjects are carefully balanced for the severity of their depression, age, sex, and so on, so that, as near as possible, we can say that we have balanced the experimental and control groups. We interview both groups two weeks later, and find that each person receiving ECT reports their condition to be reliably improved. None of the control group reports any improvement. What can we conclude? We would probably want to conclude that the procedures associated with ECT had something to do with the improvement. You might object at this point that perhaps the ECT patients received more care and attention from the nursing staff, or perhaps simply the knowledge of having ECT played a role. I deliberately stated my hypothesis in vague terms in order to lead us to this discussion. I said ECT had *something* to do with the improvement, but the question of exactly *what* would be wide open, assuming that we adopted a procedure no more rigorous than that described. The message is clear. Make your hypothesis clear and rigorous, so that, as far as we possibly can, we test *it* and no other hypothesis.

In the case of ECT, we would be likely to want to test an hypothesis of the form that ECT, by its direct electrical and biochemical effects on the patient's brain, effects an improvement in their mental state. To test such an hypothesis is more demanding, since we must try to eliminate contaminating influences; for example, that more attention is paid to ECT patients by nursing staff. Such influences are known as *confounding variables* because they confuse the issue of what is actually causing the effects on the dependent variable. We would need to have two groups treated identically except in the one respect of having, or not having, ECT. The patients in both experimental and control groups must be given an identical amount of information, so that the factor of whether they think they have received ECT cannot play a role in influencing a report of improvement. Either all must be told they did receive ECT, all told that they did not, or all left in doubt (a *blind procedure*). Since ECT requires anaesthetic, all subjects must be given this (which in itself raises fundamental problems of ethics and legality in the UK), and all must be connected to the ECT machine in the same way. The nursing staff and doctors who subsequently carry out the interviews must not know which subjects have had ECT, in case it affects their behaviour towards the patients and their expectations of success. This knowledge would be held by a researcher who only appears on the scene later (a *double-blind procedure*). As you can see, the procedures for carrying out such experimentation are of formidable difficulty. The risk of confounding variables is ever present, and yet scientific rigour demands just such stringency of testing procedures.

Another source of potential problems lies in balancing the experimental and control groups. One possible way of deciding who shall be in the control group and who in the experimental group is to allocate people (or rats) randomly to the two groups. The problem here is that what might appear to be random might not in practice be so. Suppose we have 16 cages and we order 16 male rats to put in them. We allocate cages 1–8 for the experimental rats and cages 9–16 for the control group. We keep the cages under identical conditions. When our rats arrive, we grab them 'randomly' one at a time and fill up the cages from 1–16 going from left to right in the room. Rather, we think that we take them at random, but in all probability we introduce a bias. Imagine yourself in this situation. What kind of rat would you go for as your first selection? A neurotic individual who flees from you, or a more inquisitive one that puts up no resistance to being touched? Without great care, your selection running from 1–16 would reflect an Eysenckian neuroticism scale. All of the most neurotic individuals would find themselves in the control group and all of the least neurotic would be in the experimental group. Suppose your research were on fear and stress or aggression. Such a contaminating influence could prove fatal to viable research.

SAQ 56
How might you allocate the rats in order to avoid this problem?

One possibility is to randomize your allocation. Another is to allocate the first rat chosen to cage 1, the second to cage 9, the third to cage 2, and so on. The same problem can arise in allocating students to groups. A selection on the basis of the first row in the lecture room to be allocated to the experimental group and the second row to the control group can yield undesired effects.

SAQ 57
Can you suggest why this might be so?

One way around the problem of differences between individuals is

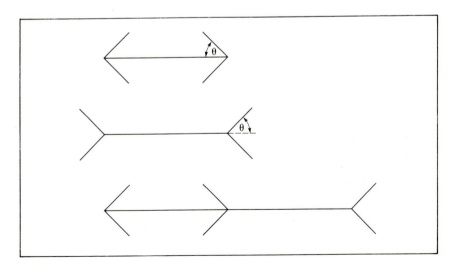

Figure 7.1   The Muller-Lyer illusion.

to use the same subjects as their own controls. Consider the psychologist's all-time favourite effect, the Muller-Lyer illusion, shown in Figure 7.1. Although the length of the two shafts is in fact the same, the shaft with inward pointing arrows looks longer than that with outward pointing arrows. Suppose we want to investigate the role of angle θ in the magnitude of the illusion. We can quantify the magnitude of the illusion by varying the length of one of the shafts until they appear to be equal in length. The extent to which we need to distort the length of the shaft from its position of true equality in order to make it appear equal to the other shaft is a measure of the magnitude of the illusion.

SAQ 58
Define the dependent and independent variables in such a test.

One possible way of doing the test would be to divide subjects into two groups, give one group the test with an angle of $30°$ and the other group an angle of $60°$. We could then compare the two groups. This would be a *between-subjects* design, because we are comparing between different subjects. An alternative way of approaching the design of the experiment would be to give each subject two tests, one at each of the two angles. This would be a *within-subjects* design, since subjects would be compared with themselves. So when do we use a within-subjects and when a between-subjects design? It is hard to give absolute hard-and-fast rules, since much depends upon experience. However, the main thing to ask is whether the subject will be seriously changed as a result of one exposure to the test. If so, go for a between-subjects design.

An example from visual perception can usefully illustrate this point. I am sure that you will be familiar with hidden-figure puzzles. For example, one is shown a picture of the Alps covered in snow, viewed from an aircraft, and asked to identify the face of Christ in the snow. A Dalmatian dog in the snow is another favourite, as is the wife/mother-in-law illusion. Suppose someone proposed that for one particular illusion, say, Christ's face in the snow, the time taken before the subject can locate the face is greatly reduced by drinking five glasses of wine. Latency was said to be reduced from a mean of 5 minutes to 10 seconds. We need to probe rigorously the validity of this claim. Clearly, it would be worthless to use the same subject with and without alcohol. Having once located the face, the whole perceptual process is so biased as to make the second test invalid as a comparison.

SAQ 59
How would we go about testing the claim?

So, where we radically alter the process under study, avoid a within-subjects design. In the case of the Muller-Lyer illusion, there is no reason to suppose that, once having looked at the arrows, one's future perception of them will be changed by the experience. Therefore we could more easily risk using a within-subjects design here. But why do we ever need to use a within-subject's design, given the risk just illustrated? There is a different risk associated with between-subject designs that is avoided by a within-subjects design, and this can also be illustrated by an example. We have spoken of random allocation of subjects between experimental and test conditions, but how can we be sure that our distribution is random in the respect that really counts? Usually, we cannot be sure. We can do our best, but we can often contaminate our study. Suppose we are looking for the effect of a drug on anxiety in rats. We would of course now take great care in not getting all of our neurotics in one group and all of the stable characters in another. But suppose neuroticism in rats were not evident in their behaviour towards a human subject. We might be dealing with animals of very different potential to display neuroticism when placed in the presence of a cat, but which show no sign of this behaviour towards us. We might then still get all the extreme neurotics in one group before we even start the experiment. This problem would be answered by testing each rat twice: once with the tranquillizer and once without.

SAQ 60
Is this a within-subjects design or a between-subjects design?

Here we need to take care again. Suppose we tested each rat with the tranquillizer, and then one week later tested it without the tranquillizer. We find that a marked difference is present. This might indeed be due to the calming effect of the tranquillizer on the first test. It could equally well mean that on the night before the final test a fox had entered the laboratory and terrified the rats all night. It could mean that rats become more neurotic as a function of age, and that the crucial age was attained between test days. To answer such objections, one would test half of the rats in the order (1) tranquillizer, (2) no tranquillizer and the other half in the order (1) no tranquillizer, (2) tranquillizer. Thus, any fox or age effects would equally influence both groups.

Answers to Self-Assessment Questions

SAQ 1

We could justify it in terms of the size of the system in question. The spectrum ranges from very large systems at the top to very small systems at the bottom. What, to a neurophysiologist, might be a component of a system (i.e. the individual nerve cell), could be the whole system of study to a biophysicist. Note that, at each level, the system is a component of the bigger system placed immediately above it.

SAQ 2

It is misleading to see one approach as being more, or less, useful. The very same phenomenon can be approached both from between- and within-disciplines. One approach will sometimes be more relevant in a given situation, depending upon the use to which we want to put the explanation.

SAQ 3

The phenomena of social interaction depend, of course, upon the characteristics of the individuals concerned, but they cannot be predicted simply on the basis of looking at individual characteristics. Phenomena of social interaction *emerge* as a result of the coming together of groups.

SAQ 4

It might seem like a trivial question, to which we are sure you answered No! However, it makes a profound point that can usefully be adapted to the study of brain and behaviour. There is a fundamental asymmetry in a system. Whereas an emergent property (in this case, beauty) can be destroyed by removing a component, beauty in no sense could be said to reside in the nose.

SAQ 5

No. There is no competition between them, since they refer to different aspects of the situation. For a comparison, suppose I say that Jones is on the 7.15 to Euston because he wants to get to Gatwick. This would not conflict with the explanation that he is on the train because his car broke down. It would, however, conflict with the assumption that he is on the 7.15 because he wants to get to Heathrow. A given question can have more than one answer, depending upon the reason for posing the question.

SAQ 6

Cells serve different functions. Nonetheless, all cells have certain properties in common, irrespective of the role that they serve. Similarly, the people making up a complex organization have certain features in common, despite serving different functions. In each case, there is a complex interdependence between the components that make up the larger system.

SAQ 7

In Morse-code we have dots and dashes, and the information is carried in this form. Action potentials are not long and short but are more or less identical, and thus equivalent, say, to the dots of Morse code. Information is coded by varying their frequency (i.e. how many of them arrive per unit of time).

SAQ 8

The eye responds to light falling on the retina. The ear responds to sounds. The taste buds of the tongue respond to chemical stimulation. The nose responds to air-borne particles. There are, of course, other possible examples.

SAQ 9

Afferent (sensory) nerve fibres enter the spinal cord via the DRN. Patient A would therefore experience loss of bodily sensations in the areas (e.g. skin) associated with the damaged neurons. The VRN carries motor (efferent) nerve fibres. Patient B would experience paralysis of the muscles supplied by these fibres.

SAQ 10

(1) Identify the changes that follow damage to the area. (2) Apply electrical or chemical stimulation to the region, and observe the outcome. (3) Record electrical activity of neurons in the area during normal function. (4) Monitor blood flow in the region.

SAQ 11

(1) Sensory cortex: involved in initial stages of processing sensory information entering the brain. (2) Motor cortex: is concerned with emitting motor commands to the muscles. (3) Association cortex: is defined in a negative way, as comprising those areas of cortex that do not receive sensory information nor are responsible for activating muscles.

SAQ 12

Sodium concentration is higher on the outside of the cell than on the inside. Therefore the concentration gradient *for sodium* will create a tendency for sodium to move from the outside to the inside.

SAQ 13

'Excess' refers to an excess of positive ions with respect to the negative ions. There is a net positive charge present.

SAQ 14

Negative ions will tend to be repelled from the inside to the outside of the cell.

SAQ 15

The influence of the concentration gradient is to move potassium from the inside of the cell to the outside. However, the influence of the potential gradient is to move it in the opposite direction, from outside to inside. These two effects don't quite cancel. Hence there is a slight movement of potassium out of the cell.

SAQ 16

(1) The forces tending to move sodium in, for example, potential gradient and sodium concentration gradient, and (2) the permeability of the membrane to sodium.

SAQ 17

The gates would be in a relatively closed state.

SAQ 18

While the potential gradient is positive, it will also tend to move potassium out of the cell. However, a bit later, on becoming negative, the potential gradient will tend to oppose the effect of the concentration gradient. Nonetheless, so long as the potential gradient is moving in a negative direction, the concentration gradient is dominant.

SAQ 19

1 = resting potential (before application of stimulus—low sodium permeability; 2 = application of depolarizing stimulus—increase in membrane permeability to sodium; 3 = membrane sodium permeability increasing still further; 4 = sudden inrush of sodium—permeability increases still further; 5 = sodium still coming in at a high rate—permeability still high; 6 = sodium gates closed. Inflow of sodium ceases (potassium permeability relatively high) potassium moving out, hence move of membrane potential in a negative direction; 7 = almost back to normal levels of sodium and potassium permeability.

SAQ 20

The refractory period (see Sect. 2.2) sets a limit to the frequency. After one action potential, a period of a few milliseconds must elapse before the cell is able to transmit another action potential.

SAQ 21

There is activity in A, B, C, and so on, but no activity at the inhibitory input side (1, 2, 3, etc.).

SAQ 22

This refers to the frequency with which the neuron transmits action potentials. A strongly excited neuron would show a relatively high frequency of action potentials.

SAQ 23

Both. These terms do not refer to a particular cell taken out of context, but to the cell with reference to a particular synapse. Thus, at synapse 1, the classical neuron provides the postsynaptic membrane at its dendrite. However, at synapse 2, this same neuron provides the presynaptic membrane (at its axon terminal).

SAQ 24

The amplitude of the response elicited decrease over the series of stimulations. If we designate the original amplitude as 100 per cent, response amplitude decreases to a value of about 20 per cent.

SAQ 25

Chemical transmitter is released by the arrival of an action potential. It migrates across the synaptic gap and influences the postsynaptic membrane.

SAQ 26

The response magnitude again decreases as the stimulation is repeated. Such habituation of a system that has already been habituated once, and then shown a revival, is known as 'rehabituation'.

SAQ 27

Both spontaneous recovery and dishabituation refer to a revival of response amplitude in an habituated system. In the former, the revival comes about simply as a result of a period free from stimulation. Time is what influences responsiveness. For dishabituation, a stimulus extraneous to the habituated system plays the role of reviving the system.

SAQ 28

Even more calcium channels have been opened up than were originally open.

SAQ 29

No. The response is of the same magnitude as before habituation in this particular case.

SAQ 30

A spot of light that completely fills the excitatory centre (ON region), but does not invade the surrounding inhibitory OFF region.

SAQ 31

That as well as there being excitatory connections to the ganglion cell, there are inhibitory connections. Light falling on a population of receptors corresponding to the ON region causes excitation of the ganglion cell. Conversely, light that activates receptors in the OFF region causes inhibition to be exerted onto the ganglion cell.

SAQ 32

Because the image falls upon both excitatory and inhibitory regions of the receptive field. Hence excitatory and inhibitory effects tend to cancel. By contrast, the light annulus falls exclusively upon the excitatory ON annular region. There would be no inhibition exerted by the OFF centre region, since 'darkness' falls there.

SAQ 33

The nociceptor detects tissue damage. Activity of the nociceptor is the first stage of a complex process that usually leads to the sensation of pain. However, the relationship between tissue damage and pain is a complex one, involving several stages of processing. Hence, it is misleading to refer to nociceptors as pain receptors, since pain is not something that is 'detected' or 'received' but is a property of the whole system. By analogy, receptors in the retina detect the presence of light. This is the first stage of a process that might involve detection of a visual form (i.e. perception). However, numerous other stagess of processing are involved. The relationship between the light stimulus and what is ultimately perceived is not a simple one.

SAQ 34

There are a number of possible sites of intervention that one might consider. First, the substance might prevent activation of the nociceptor by the stimulus. One could try preventing or hindering *initiation* of the action potential. Second, a substance might prevent transmission of the action potential along the axon of the nociceptor. Third, the substance might work by preventing the nociceptor from activating the cell in the spinal cord that transmits noxious information to the brain. One could try blocking the synapse itself by introducing a substance that prevents synaptic transmission.

SAQ 35

After visiting the dentist you might have had a numb mouth for a while. Lignocaine tends to affect not only the nociceptors but also sensory neurons carrying innocuous information.

SAQ 36

The UCS is the snake. The UCR is the fear reaction evoked by the snake. The CS is the house, and the CR is the fear evoked by the house. By means of classical conditioning, an otherwise innocuous object, the house, acquires a fear-eliciting potency.

SAQ 37

Remove the food pellets from the delivery apparatus so that the rat does not get reinforced for bar-pressing. The rat would be said to be extinguished when it no longer presses the bar.

SAQ 38

Remove the snake. The index of when the conditioned response had extinguished would be when the child no longer shows signs of fear on approaching the house (this example is given to illustrate the principle of classical conditioning. You should not assume that extinction is always a simple matter).

SAQ 39

One possibility might be to try releasing it in a T-maze, where it must make a decision as to which side to take at the junction. One characteristic visual stimulus at an arm in the maze could be associated with a period of stroking when the animal arrives at the goal-box. Another stimulus at the choice point could be associated with an outcome of no-stroking. If stroking is a positive reinforcer, we would expect to see an increase in the frequency with which the animal takes the arm having a stimulus characteristic predicting stroking. If, however, stroking is a punishment we would expect to see a decline in the frequency with which the animal takes this side.

SAQ 40

It could constitute either, depending upon the contingency in operation. If the loud noise is presented when the animal performs a certain response, then it is being used in a punishment contingency. However, if the animal can escape from the loud sound by performing a certain response, it is being used in a negative reinforcement contingency.

SAQ 41

The teacher doubtless sees being sent out of the class as a form of punishment, an aversive event that, it is supposed, will cause a decrease in the frequency of the disruptive behaviour. From the child's point of view it is more likely to constitute positive or negative reinforcement. Throwing the missile is followed by escape from the aversive stimulus (learning French) and attainment of freedom. The former is the negative reinforcement aspect, and the latter is the positive reinforcement aspect.

SAQ 42

The amount of solution ingested after an aversive encounter associated with a visual stimulus, as compared to the amount ingested after an equivalent encounter associated with a taste stimulus. The greater the degree of association, the less of the solution the animal will be prepared to ingest.

SAQ 43

The unconditional reaction of the animal is sickness. The conditional reaction, shown to subsequent presentation of the solution that had been ingested prior to sickness, is one of avoidance. Clearly, sickness and avoidance of a solution are not identical reactions, but it is useful to consider the avoidance to be a part of the overall negative reaction that was aroused initially.

SAQ 44

Six seconds.

SAQ 45

Either model could predict the phenomenon of retrograde amnesia. However, *shrinkage* of retrograde amnesia favours one of the models (see main text that follows).

SAQ 46

It would prevent the formation of memory; that is to say, the animal should show no sign (or a reduced sign) of having learned the task that had been set. The animal would be compared in its learning ability with a control animal being injected with a substance not having this effect. One would then be in a position to see the reduced learning ability.

SAQ 47

Sometimes we show eagerness to drink and at other times experience satiety. It depends to a large extent upon the amount of water in the body. A deficiency of body fluids accentuates the motivation to drink. A surplus of body fluids diminishes the motivation.

SAQ 48

It would be expected to drink considerably more on the second occasion, since we have removed the restraining influence of short-term feedback.

SAQ 49

Mind as an epiphenomenon is unable to influence the physical body. By contrast, in Descartes' dualistic model, mental events are able to influence physical processes in the body.

SAQ 50

It would suggest that it is more useful to examine brain events. Mental events are the mere passive translation of the physical brain events. Their study might well be interesting but could not yield answers of much practical significance.

SAQ 51

Perhaps the first point that such a theorist would make is that both Jones and Brown could be right. It is possible that they are both describing the very same events in two different languages. Brown is using brain language and Jones is using mind language.

SAQ 52

To such a theorist, Bill's claim would constitute a viable piece of evidence: a description in terms of subjective feelings. Such a theorist would assume that corresponding to Bill's anger there exist brain events. One could look for the translation between the mental state of feeling angry and the corresponding brain events, but the latter does not provide a better or more accurate account. Which account one would give depends upon the purpose of the explanation.

SAQ 53

In neither model would one say that the mental state *caused* the brain state. Mind as epiphenomenon is unable to exert an influence on the physical body. In identity theory, mental events are identical to their corresponding brain events. As such one does not cause the other.

SAQ 54

Our experimental hypothesis would be that the amount drunk increases as a function of the length of prior deprivation. The independent variable is the number of hours of water deprivation. The dependent variable is the amount of water that the rats drink.

SAQ 55

The independent variable is the time that elapses between presentation of the syllable and the time that recall is prompted. The dependent variable is the ability to recall.

SAQ 56

You could try cutting up 16 bits of paper, putting the numbers 1 to 16 on them, and then just after each rat is taken, pulling a number out of a hat. The number determines the cage to which the rat should be allocated.

SAQ 57

The possibilities for contamination are many. Perhaps all the extraverts sit on the front row, and the introverts fill up the rows nearer the back. Perhaps the front row fills up last and hence gets the late-comers who have problems leaving the bar.

SAQ 58

The independent variable is the angle of the fins in the figure. The dependent variable is the magnitude of the illusion. The hypothesis is that the latter depends upon the former.

SAQ 59

Use two groups of naive subjects, matched as well as we can for age, sex, vision, religious experience (yes! experimentation is tough).

SAQ 60

Within-subjects.

Bibliography

Brown, R. E. and McFarland, D. J. (1979) 'Interaction of hunger and sexual motivation in the male rat: a time-sharing approach', *Animal Behaviour*, 27, 887–96.

Cabanac, M. and Russek, M. (1982) *'Régulation et contrôle en biologie*, Quebec, Les Presses de L'Université Laval.

Dickinson, A. (1980) *'Contemporary Animal Learning Theory*', Cambridge, Cambridge University Press.

Epstein, A. (1982) 'Instinct and motivation as explanations for complex behaviour', in *The Physiological Mechanisms of Motivation*, D. W. Pfaff (ed.), New York, Springer, pp. 25–58.

Garcia, J., Clarke, J. C. and Hankins, W. G. (1973) 'Natural responses to scheduled rewards', in *Perspectives in Ethology*, P. P. G. Bateson and P. H. Klopfer (eds.), New York, Plenum Press, pp. 1–41.

Greene, J. and Hicks, C. (1984) *Basic Cognitive Processes*, Milton Keynes, Open University Press.

Hardy, J. D. and Stolwijk, J. A. J. (1968) in *Medical Physiology*, V. B. Mountcastle (ed.), 12th edn, St Louis, Mosby.

Hebb, D. O. (1949) *The Organization of Behaviour*, New York, Wiley.

Hubel, D. and Wiesel, T. N. (1959) 'Receptive fields of single neurons in the cat's striate cortex', *Journal of Physiology*, 148, 574–91.

Kandel, E. R. and Schwartz, J. H. (1982) 'Molecular biology of learning: modulation of transmitter release', *Science*, 218, 433–43.

LeMagnen, J. (1985) *Hunger*, Cambridge, Cambridge University Press.

Lewis, D. (1979) 'Psychobiology of active and inactive memory', *Psychological Bulletin*, 86, 1054–83.

Olds, J. (1958) 'Self-stimulation of the brain', *Science*, 127, 315–24.

Rolls, E. (1975) *The Brain and Reward*, Oxford, Pergamon.

Rose, S. P. R. (1976) *The Conscious Brain*, Harmondsworth, Penguin Books.

—— (1981) 'What should a biochemistry of learning and memory be about?' *Neuroscience*, 6, 811–21.

—— (1984) 'Strategies in studying the cell biology of learning and memory', in L. R. Squire and N. Butters (eds.) *Neuropsychology of Memory*, New York, Guildford Press, pp. 547–54.

Skinner, B. F. (1973) *Beyond Freedom and Dignity*, Harmondsworth: Penguin.

Squire, L. R. and Cohen, N. J. (1984) 'Human memory and amnesia', in *The Neurobiology of Learning and Memory*, J. L. McGaugh, G. Lynch and N. M. Weinberger (eds), pp. 3–64, New York, Guildford Press.

Toates, F. M. (1986) *Motivational Systems*, Cambridge, Cambridge University Press.

—— and Oatley, K. (1970) 'Computer simulation of thirst and water balance', *Medical and Biological Engineering*, 8, 71–87.

Index of Concepts